GIVE POWER TO THE PEOPLE!:

The Congregational Enablement-Model Revisited

SESA WO SUBAN
"Change or transform your character "
symbol of life transformation

This symbol combines two separate adinkra symbols, the "Morning Star" which can mean a new start to the day, placed inside the wheel, representing rotation or independent movement.

GIVE POWER TO THE PEOPLE!:
The Congregational Enablement-Model Revisited

by Alvin C. Bernstine

© 2013 Alvin C. Bernstine

Published by ACB Ministry @ Bethlehem Missionary Baptist Church
684 Juliga Woods Street
Richmond, CA 94804

ISBN 978-0-9767020-2-5

Dedication

To the three wonderful congregations that loved me enough to call me, "Pastor', and believed in me enough to trust me with the work of making disciples of Jesus Christ, even as I struggled to empower them to do ministry.

Olivet Baptist Church - Nashville, Tennessee

Mount Lebanon Baptist Church - Brooklyn, New York

Bethlehem Missionary Baptist Church - Richmond, California

CONTENTS

PREFACE 13

I. INTRODUCTION: 27
   Why We Must Give Power to the People

II. SOME ASSUMPTIONS THAT GUIDE THE TASK: 37
    A Theology for Giving Power to the People

III. DEFINING THE TASK: 55
     Clarifying the Power Given to the People

IV. HINDRANCES THAT DISABLE CONGREGATIONS..............67
    AND HINDER CHRISTIAN EDUCATION: Identifying
    Challenges to Giving Power to the People

V. THE CONGREGATIONAL-ENABLEMENT MODEL: 83
   A Model that Gives Power to the People

VI. DIRECTION FOR THE CONGREGATIONAL.......................99
    ENABLEMENT MODEL: Shaping a Person who Gives
    Power to the People

VII. ORGANIZATION: 107
     The Plan for Giving Power to the People

VIII. IMPLEMENTATION OF CHRISTIAN EDUCATION...............121
      ACTIVITIES: Giving Power to the People Where They Are

IX. INTRODUCING TO THE CONGREGATION 133
    THE ADVENTURE OF CHRISTIAN EDUCATION: Giving
    Power to the People

X.	EXPENSE AND EVALUATION:...141 Evaluating the Power of the People	
XI.	PREACHING SERMONS ON CHRISTIAN EDUCATION:.....151 Preaching as A Means of Empowerment	
XII.	BIBLE STUDY FOR CHRISTIAN EDUCATION: ....161 Teaching to Give Power to the People	
XIII.	APPENDICES 175	
	APPENDIX A	
	APPENDIX B	
	APPENDIX C	
	APPENDIX D	
	APPENDIX E	
	APPENDIX F	
	APPENDIX G	
	APPENDIX H	

FOREWORD TO FIRST PUBLICATION

Thank God for the opportunity to share with those who read this book. It has been mine to observe this writer as a believer in Christ and a student in many schools and colleges of Christian education.

Alvin Bernstine is a good Bible student and has based the contents of this book on sound biblical principles. It will be well for Christian workers and leaders in Christian education to read and reread this book and put into practice these proven principles of spiritual leadership.

I also believe this book can serve well as a guide for leaders to use in training others. A crisis of leadership engulfs the world. Political leaders, economic experts, editorial writers, newsmen and spokesmen in the field of education and religion raise the huge cry: "Men who know the way and can lead others in the right path of Christian education are few."

The writer of this book sets forth ways of developing an effective Department of Christian Education in the local church for adults, young adults and children. The Christian church today, as never before, is greatly in need of well trained leaders. We must be aware that leadership comes in many varieties, good and bad; effective and ineffective; positive and negative; right and wrong.

We need to look at leadership from the standpoint of the Bible. Both Old and New Testament are alive with eternal truths that bear witness on the subject. The teachings of Jesus Christ Himself burst forth in clear and understandable principles. Analysis and application of these biblical teachings are the aims of the writer.

It is generally recognized that the objectives of Christian education and the objectives of the church are, and should be, the same. The task for the Christian church, for example, is to bring children, young men and adults into a vital and personal relationship with God through Jesus Christ, and to enlist them into the work of the Kingdom of Heaven.

This is precisely the objectives of Christian education. As this idea is developed, it becomes increasingly clear that the task of Christian education is identical with the task of Christian religion. In this sense, Christian education takes its rightful place as a method or instrument by which individuals and society are brought in a saving knowledge of Jesus Christ.

This book goes forth with the prayer that God will use it to increase the ranks of men and women who will provide leadership true to the Word of God, faithful to Jesus Christ and committed to the work and will of God.

    Abraham H. Newman, Pastor
    Bethlehem Baptist Church
    Richmond, California

ACKNOWLEDGEMENT

Years ago the late Dr. Benjamin Elijah Mays, past president of Morehouse College, surmised that his contributions were the result of nameless people "who pushed him." The names of those who have encouraged the revisiting of this work are too numerous to cite. Suffice it to say that the hard working people of the National Baptist Convention USA, Inc., particularly those of the National Baptist Congress of Christian Education, have pushed me.

I am especially proud to have as a personal friend, mentor, and colleague, the Reverend Dr. Elliott Cuff, who currently serves as Congress President. Dr. J. Alfred Smith, Sr., Pastor Emeritus of the Allen Temple Baptist Church, Oakland, California has believed in me for over 30 years. His indelible impact on the black church life is legend.

I am appreciative to the creative genius of Joyce Evans, who provides such remarkable assistance in preparing my manuscripts for publication. In the words of the compassionate Rugrats, you are the "bestest." Finally, I want to thank my immediate family, particularly my siblings for honoring my life with your undying love and support. My "Big Sister", Shirlee Zipporah, remains a constant source of inspiration. I love you all!

GIVE POWER TO THE PEOPLE!
THE CONGREGATIONAL-ENABLEMENT MODEL REVISITED

(Originally Published as
HOW TO ORGANIZE A DEPARTMENT OF CHRISTIAN EDUCATION
WITHIN THE LOCAL BAPTIST CHURCH:
A CONGREGATIONAL ENABLEMENT MODEL)

PREFACE

I can't believe it! It has been over twenty-five years since the original publication of this work, and twenty years since the revised publication. It has been totally unexpected, but after twenty-five years the continued demand for practical assistance has made this little publication a denominational best seller among the masses who are serious about Christian education within the National Baptist Convention, USA, Inc. I am in awe at the eager responses to my grappling attempt to make sense out of what I tried to do in my first stipend position at the Westwood Baptist Church-University Center, Nashville, Tennessee. The continuing demand of Baptists and others to use the book has motivated me to revisit and rethink the task of doing Christian education within the local church. After twenty-five years I consider it a privilege to further explore the incredible assignment of making disciples through Christian education.

Needless to say, much has changed in the world and much has changed within the life of the church, although much about church life remains the same. Indeed, there have been changes within the slow-to-change traditional church, and I have had my share of personal and professional changes. It is clear that we are at a critical juncture in history and we face some unusual and unprecedented challenges. No one can responsibly minister any relevant Christian ministry without considering some of the vast and diverse issues that affect the people of our churches.

External to the church has been a potpourri of social and political realities that have radically altered the world to which we are called to provide a witness. We have to acknowledge that Postmodernism has reshaped the way the world is viewed. Although the use of the term "postmodern" does not find regular usage in the average local congregation, its impact profoundly shapes every parishioner. Postmodernism is a reaction against the values that once shaped our world but are no longer operative in the modern worldview. The key characteristics of Postmodernism are:

- The centrality of community
- The primacy of experience
- The subjectivity of truth – truth is relative
- The complexity of human perception
- The fragility of progress
- The unreality of absolutes
- The enormity of the spiritual

- The plurality of worldviews[1]

None of us can deny how profoundly September 11, 2001 has painfully reshaped the way we live in the world. The landscapes of travel, communication, commerce, and community have been radically altered by the horrific tragedy of September 11. Without a doubt two terms of an impeached president, William Jefferson Clinton; two terms of a near impotent president, George W. Bush, and the election and reelection of America's first African American President, Barak Hussein Obama, has all radically reshaped the way the world relates to America.

"None of us can deny how profoundly September 11, 2001 has painfully reshaped the way we live in the world."

We are currently retreating from two wars with an unidentified enemy and a radically reshaped foreign policy. Our reaction to September 11 pulled the United States into futilely trying to reshape the governments of two anti-Western countries. Many of us are struggling to accept the eerie fact that presidential elections can be secured through suspect means and that wars can be waged under false pretenses.

The altering of global economics that threaten the security of the middle class is more than just some passing economic fluctuation. In 2008-09 we experienced the

---

1 Creps, Earl, *Discipling in a Postmodern World*, Enrichment Journal: A Journal for Pentecostal Ministry, Apr., 2004, p. 2.

Give Power to the People!

most devastating economic downturn since the Great Depression. Millions of hard-working Americans lost homes through a ruthless assemblage of unregulated marketing gimmicks. Currently, real deals are being made that really affect how people will live in a growing world of shrinking resources. Corporate greed and deceitful stock scandals have been paid for by the most vulnerable. No one can ignore the fact that the world has changed.

Technologically the world has been made to seem more efficient. In the past twenty-five years computers have become permanent fixtures in most of our lives. When I wrote the first manuscript of this work, I used a portable typewriter. The second was done on a desktop computer, and I now prepare this one on a small notebook that has more capacity than the previous two combined. The computer tablets have made my notebook obsolete. Amazingly, I will upload this document on the Internet and send it to an editor, who will then send it back to me. A digital publisher will format, bind, and produce the finished product in less than a week. I will never have a single face-to-face meeting throughout this whole publishing process. Wow! We are truly living in a different world.

There have also been changes within Christendom. Denominationalism has hit the brick wall of reality and has suffered major damages in support and relevance. Church growth specialist C. Peter Wagner described the church as living in "Post-denominationalism." Whatever we call it, the handwriting is on the wall. There is not a major denomination in America that is not being challenged to redefine its mission and purpose. Most so-called mainline denominations are stagnant and stunned by the growing disinterest of once loyal denominational

> *"...the traditional church is often viewed as a dull oddity within Christendom."*

churches. The National Baptist Convention, USA, Inc. was traumatized by scandal and had to painfully witness an affable President being convicted and sentenced to prison. The past president, Dr. William J. Shaw, was instrumental in providing leadership that helped recover the integrity of the convention. However, many within the ranks of our churches have never attended a denominational function and have little interest in doing so. The state of denominations is clearly in flux.

The current emphasis on self-gratification within many churches does little to motivate denominational interest, particularly among the average parishioners. Also, the rise of mega-church ministries has greatly challenged the meager efforts of aging, obsolete, and over-worked denominational agencies. Mega-churches have challenged us to consider targeting ministries to certain specific groups, such as Men's Ministry, Women's Ministry, Youth Ministry, Singles' Ministry, etc. The rising numbers of specialized conferences have replaced many denominational gatherings. Also, thoughtless neo-Pentecostalism has seized the traditional church in every denomination. Many are inclined to celebration as the highest expression of their walk with God. As a result, the traditional church is often viewed as a dull oddity within Christendom.

The publication of The Purpose-Driven Church, by Rick Warren, a white Baptist preacher, has had an indelible impact on Protestant churches world-wide. It has been absolutely mind- boggling how many leading African American leaders have been influenced by this publication, often without thought to serious cultural distinctions. Without a doubt, Rick Warren's insightful analysis of congregational systems, assisted by numerous biblical references, provides an easy reference for the searching-for-answers local pastor. Pastor Warren's incredible success at growing a "purpose-driven" mega church enhanced his standing among church leaders. Moreover, the discipleship component of a Purpose-Driven church complements the task of Christian education. No serious Christian educator can afford to ignore the impact of Warren's publication, whether or not he or she agrees or disagrees with its findings.

The growing number of women in pulpits, even serving as pastors in major congregations, challenges the traditional approaches to ministry. A woman provided sterling leadership over one of the largest gatherings of African American ministers in the country, the Hampton Ministers' Conference. It does not matter how one feels about women in ministry, the fact remains: women are in the pulpit to stay. Currently there are more women securing seminary education than men, which raises serious questions about who will be most qualified to lead the church in the new millennium. How we engage in the ministry of Christian education must reflect the signs of the times.

I am honored to be able to once again contribute to the challenge of providing Christian education in the local church. I see my task as continuing what I began in the first publication, which is to assist the local church in the making of effective disciples for Jesus Christ. I see within my assignment the task of assisting churches in the process of developing meaningful ministries that reflect an awareness of what is happening in the world.

Central to this continuing work is sensitivity to the language currently being used to advance the cause of Christ. No one can deny that language serves as a serious component of how we view reality. There is no such thing as innocent language. Language is a product of culture and has always been loaded with ideologies. It is widely known that language shapes the political, social, and even spiritual agendas of our world. How we speak about a reality determines how we relate to that reality.

At this junction in history I believe that the use of the term "Department of Christian Education" does not serve us well. The term "department" seems to isolate and give rise to a hierarchical construct. The use of hierarchical language does not advance the vision of relationships as espoused in scripture, nor does it serve well among people who yearn for meaningful relationships, particularly those with a legacy of oppression. Thus, in this publication the term "department" will give way to the more biblical and relational term "ministry." After continued demands for and questions about the absence of the flow chart, I bring back a modified version of it. I would only caution the

Give Power to the People!

> *"The preacher who can teach will develop people who can reach beyond the comfort zones of the status quo."*

reader to view it as a tool and not a portrait of hierarchical church arrangement.

I also see it as my task to include more practical ways to integrate meaningful Bible study into the life of the local church. People are yearning for ways to understand how an ancient book intersects with modern lives. The growing publications addressing relevant ways in which the Bible impacts life are a testimony to the need among believers. Currently, there are more people interested in Bible study than I can ever recall in my Christian life. As a consequence, the continuing study of the Bible is a real need in most churches. A relevant ministry of Christian education must address this very critical need.

After twenty-five plus years of trying to preach every Sunday, I am also aware of how preaching can be a powerful tool for teaching. The preacher who can teach will develop people who can reach beyond the comfort zones of the status quo. Thus, I include some suggestions on how the preaching moment can become a teaching moment.

The inclusion of discussion questions at the conclusion of each chapter should provide opportunity for reflection and healthy group interaction. It is the goal of the discussion questions to engage people further into the

The Congregational Enablement-Model Revisited

enablement mode of intentional disciple-making. People talking in healthy relationships represent one of the most empowering things we can do.

Again, I am honored to be able to continue a work that I began as a young pastor. After nearly thirty years of pastoral ministry within the local church I now see better what I once speculated about. I not only see better, but I better understand where people really are in the pursuit of becoming disciples of Jesus Christ. Moreover, I am also acutely aware of what works and what does not work within the current scene of the church.

As a consequence, the revision of this work will be rather extensive. I hold to the basic substance of the previous publications, but I will make significant changes within the major components of the manuscript and provide some helpful additions. I pray that the focus of the book will remain and the continuing use of this publication will further the work that we hold dear – making disciples for Risen Lord. "Let us not grow weary in well-doing."

PREFACE TO REVISED EDITION

As I reread the preface of the initial publication, I was stunned by its continuing relevance. So moved was I that I really saw no need to add to it, other than to state the revisions and to smooth out the rough edges of my apprenticeship grammar. Although the overwhelming demand for the republishing of this book is a wonderful surprise, I believe the original preface states adequately any reasons I might have for revisiting this work. I only hope that the revisions compliment the maturity of our mutual growth.

Chapter 1 represents the major revision of the book. This is a new chapter, which sets forth the primary assumptions that should guide the work of Christian education. I really present a theology of Christian education, without the normal jargon of the theology. Chapter 2 briefly introduces the task. The task is presented by using biblical paradigms as guides for Christian education. This chapter also has some significant revisions. In chapter 3 the task of Christian education is defined. A comprehensive definition of Christian education is offered, with significant revisions and additions. Chapter 4 defines the Congregational Enablement Model. This chapter has also been revised, for it reflects my continued quest to better the work of Christian education. The remaining chapters are essentially the same as the first edition.

The bibliography has also been revised to reflect some current developments in Christian education, as well as some recent works that have impacted the author. The

The Congregational Enablement-Model Revisited

appendices remain to illustrate certain important facets of the task. Admittedly, I thought to delete the sermons from this edition, until an aspirant of Christian education used one of the sermons to jolt the sensitivities of a congregation. I witnessed the impact of her quotes from one sermon upon that particular congregation and I was convicted to retain the sermons with slight revisions.

PREFACE TO FIRST EDITION

The Pauline burden of observing his people "perish because of a lack of knowledge" speaks adequately toward answering the question of why this writing. The "zeal of God" apparent among Black Baptists is so often "not according to knowledge." My life-long relationship with National Baptists has witnessed increased irrelevancies, unnerving fruitlessness, and needless instances of spiritual fatalities. Our people have, for too long, missed out on the blessings of informed discipleship. One of the major reasons for such a void has been the mischievous antics of racism. The dominant culture's historical efforts to educationally deprive Blacks still unveil ugly scars. Slavery, institutional racism, and miseducation yet hold many within socioeconomic walls. Our people (Black Baptists) represent a massive extension of the multitude.

Another equally sinister reason has been our own blatant neglect. Many have been the opportunities for us to better our people, but we have neglected them for selfish reasons. The task of equipping our people has been foolishly placed in the hands of a non-religious public school system. The Black church has done some things well, but addressing the task of equipping persons for faithful Christian discipleship has been minimal. Most of our congregations are dying as the direct result of an uninformed, disinterested leadership structure. The Black Baptist Church is one of the few denominations, out of more than 260,000, that allow persons to lead without training. Anyone can pick up a Bible, "holler" once or twice, and lead Black Baptist. Responsible discipleship has been grossly neglected among the average grass-root congregation.

The times no longer allow us the luxury of such neglect. Although my pastoral responsibilities are immense, I have paused to patch together an effort to help National Baptists. This effort has been quilted from the fabrics of my own struggle to disciple the Lord's people. In a step-by-step method, I present a model to be profitably practiced.

This model originated as a humble effort to organize a Department of Christian Education with the Westwood Baptist Church - University Center, Nashville, Tennessee. I was but a student, yet Dr. Amos Jones, Jr., gave me this huge assignment. Since then the project has continued as an effort to address the larger needs of the Black Baptist community. The belief behind this writing is: every local church has disciple-making possibilities. Every congregation, with God's help, can become an enablement station. The primary task of every congregation is to enable those who follow Him, to effectively follow Him.

Chapter 1 briefly introduces the task. Using biblical paradigms as guides for the task, the work is presented. Chapter 2 defines the task. A comprehensive definition of Christian education is suggested. Chapter 3 defines the model/approach being suggested. Chapter 4 deals with the development of a disciple-making director. Chapter 5 offers an organizational plan for an effective ministry/board of Christian education. Chapter 6 describes a method of implementing a new life-giving approach to

Give Power to the People!

Christian education. Chapter 7 shares an approach to introducing the ministry to the congregation. The "nuts and bolts" of a successful ministry of Christian education are dealt with in Chapters 8 and 9. The chapters are to be read in sequence. Included in this book is a very helpful annotated bibliography, which enhances further study. Also, I have included some illustrative appendices. As inspirational reading, I have also included a few "preached" sermons on Christian education.

My prayer is that the Black Baptist church experiences a renewal of the Holy Spirit, as it responsibly aligns her program with the will of the Holy Spirit. Jesus is still calling for His followers to "make disciples" of all persons, especially our own.

I. Introduction

Why We Must Give Power to the People

The greatest accomplishment and honor that we can award our churches is the formation and development of viable ministries of Christian Education. Our accomplishment would be great because of the apparent void in most churches having relevant and attractive Christian education concerns. Most of our churches barely offer impressive church schools, let alone any ongoing ministry of Christian training and nurture. In most Black Baptist churches the once vibrant program known as Baptist Training Union has been lost and was temporarily replaced with a weak and woeful replacement known as the Nurture for Baptist Churches. Our "sister" conventions don't even have the Nurture program, and their Congresses of Christian Education are pitifully weak and inconsequential. Thus, a worthwhile accomplishment for any congregation would be to develop a consistent and intentional educational ministry. Such a ministry can be realized through the creative development of a Ministry of Christian Education.

A functioning Ministry of Christian Education awards qualitative honor to any congregation that embraces this honorable mission. The local church that prioritizes Christian Education leaps in the direction of quality fulfillment of the Christian mission. It is without question that the Lord expects us to do our best; and we can do our best, give our best, and be our best only when we put forth that we "know" what is best. In fact, there are immeasurable faith possibilities latent within most of our churches, which can only be realized through the dynamic powers created through a ministry of Christian education.

"A worthwhile accomplishment for any congregation would be to develop a consistent and intentional educational ministry."

The needs within our communities have become almost overwhelming. All of our churches need to do more than we are currently doing. There are no substitutes for the types of ministries a local church could conceivably create once it becomes passionately involved in the work of Christian education. Moreover, we must unreservedly assert that some form of

Christian education may well be the only means of church work that offers us a quality path toward our desired end - making disciples for Jesus Christ.

Since the "making of disciples" constitutes the ultimate goal of our local churches, we must facilitate that end through consistent and creative expressions of Christian education. We must allow God to stretch us beyond the places of the ordinary and move us to experience the extraordinary. Christian education provides us a foolproof program for getting ordinary people to do extraordinary ministry. Thus, there should be no end to our desire to gird our churches with powerful ministries of Christian education.

First, Christian education must also be intentional and insightful. It has been stated that "what we don't do naturally, we must do intentionally." There has to be an intentional approach to ministry that leads people to insightful expressions of faith. God's commands to Moses' Israel not only gave keen insight into the nature of God's love but also provided Israel opportunities to experience incredible expressions of faith. Christian education can empower the normal ministries of the church into incredible moments of revelation and inspiration.

Second, those who engage in Christian education provide people with tools for the rigorous and enriching journey of faith. The journey of the faithful requires special tools, faith capacity and perspective to embrace what is often a tedious journey. No one serves God well who does not have moments of trials and difficulties. The church does well to equip its people for the total life of faith, which includes mountains high and valleys low. Jesus spent much of His earthly ministry in preparing the disciples for His crucifixion, in order for them to better understand and appropriate His resurrection. The Resurrection defines what the Christian faith is all about, but the Crucifixion gives sobering insight on the social context in which the Christian faith must live. All who dare live in the power of the resurrection will inevitably deal with the gory of the crucifixion.

Third, it is always our hope that even the mystery of the faith can be approached in ways that are practical and promising. In this "how-to" culture, the church can ill afford to be abstract and ethereal, outdated and obsolete. We can learn much from the wisdom of those immersed in popular religion. It helps us when we know that "popular religion in America is that dominant brand of religion, carried and shaped by the mass media, which confirms and strengthens the values the viewing, listening, and reading public already holds dear. It is packaged and sold in a technological how-to-do-it form and is communicated to bored and anxiety-ridden individuals by appealing celebrities."[2]

Fourth, it is helpful to us to know that we must provide people with practical approaches that lead to the promising hope of a life in Christ. Such an approach must be ever mindful of the cultural and contextual realities that impinge upon people. We have to be convinced that Christian education provides the means of teaching

---

2 *Quebedeaux, Richard, By What Authority: The Rise of Personality Cults in America, Harper & Row, Publishers, San Francisco, 1982, p. 16.*

The Congregational Enablement-Model Revisited

"all persons" the fulfilling life, uniquely discovered in Jesus Christ. I believe Christian education gives us a path, uniquely ours, toward participating in meaningful kingdom building enterprises. Without such an engaging challenge, all other peripheral concerns are doomed to either eternal frustrations or idolatrous prostrations.

Most serious church leaders could endlessly enumerate reasons for our acceptance of the challenge of Christian education. Although the purpose of this writing is not to enumerate the various and serious reasons for a passionate leap into the riches of Christian Education, nonetheless, we must be alerted that the "times" deny us the prodigious liberty of any other trite concerns. It's an overused cliché, and certainly has its flaws, but it does hold that we have been busy majoring in the minors and minoring in the majors. We must be about the liberating business of Christian education. We must elevate Christian education from the hollowed echoes of mere suggestions, denominational posturing and campaign rhetoric, to the substantive reaches of engaging action. Simply put, we must quit talking about Christian education and start doing Christian education.

Finally, Christian education is more than vocalizing words. It is more than empty rhetoric espoused by the intellectually pompous or the academically insecure. We have too many people bluffing good people out of powerful witnessing by posturing intellectual and ecclesiastical superiority. We have to see that Christian education is really about enabling people to better understand the Word, so that they may better manifest God's Word in our world. It's about giving power to the people. Moreover, we must remove Christian education from the agenda of low priority and place it foremost on our churches' agendas in qualitative time, quantitative financial expenditures, and resounding communicative emphases. Christian education must move to a primary place in our churches' lives, or we assist in making meaningless the faith in the often backward lives of powerless and pitiful parishioners.

Having briefly stated some sense of the urgency that promotes this writing, I now move toward stating its primary objective. The intent of this presentation is to offer afresh a viable model for the development of a lively Ministry of Christian Education. The model that I propose utilizes an approach I have coined the "Congregational-Enablement Model." The term "Congregational-Enablement" is uniquely used in this writing, but it seems to be the prevailing approach used by Jesus and the early church. Jesus sought to enable "all persons" in the process of becoming whole persons. His ministry was summarized in His own words: "I came that you might have life and have it more abundantly."[3] I will attempt to better define the approach below, but for now I seek only

> *"Christian education must move to a primary place in our churches' lives, or we assist in making meaningless the faith in the often backward lives of powerless and pitiful parishioners."*

---

3   John 10:10

to introduce it. It is my belief that the "Congregational-Enablement Model" seeks to address the unique and "peculiar" features of the local church and is particularly relevant to the African American Church.

Within the African American church there exist fertile grounds for the congregational approach, primarily because of the congregational dynamics of the African American Church and a legacy of communal disempowerment. Someone has stated that there is no greater expression of democracy than within the African American church, even among those who purport theocratic government. An example is when a particular African American church within Methodism took a congregational stance against the Methodist tradition to move its pastor. It threatened the denomination that it did not have to be a Methodist church if the Methodist powers-that-be sought to remove its pastor. Needless to say, the church's position was viewed as the wiser one for the sake of denominational peace.

It is hard to argue against the power of the congregation when we consider that most African American Baptist churches are thoroughly congregational. Baptist Churches do not claim to be congregational in a purely denominational sense, but in a political sense. The congregation ultimately determines the life-flow of our churches, particularly the powerful undercurrents of influence and direction. No single person, pastor or otherwise, can single-handedly lift and carry a heavy and obstinate congregation. Like it or not, if the congregation does not desire change, no substantive changes ever occur. If the congregation insists on not moving, movement rarely takes place. Therefore, the Congregational-Enablement approach seeks to strategically exploit those unique and "peculiar" features of the local Baptist congregation, and wherever else possible.

I want to "walk on the waters" of a possible difficulty and assert that it matters not how large or small, complex or simple a congregation may be - this model works! The Congregational-Enablement approach can lead any congregation toward realizing the "milk and honey" within the Promised Land of Christian education. We often hear the impotent assertion, "just because it works in one church, it doesn't necessarily have to work in another." Such an assertion may possess marginal elements of truth. However, sometimes this statement is made to veil ignorance and inadequacies, and to avoid challenge and responsibility. Some things don't work in all churches! What works in one congregation does not have to work the way it worked in another congregation. But all of our congregations need a viable educational ministry. We must avoid ignoring critical needs because of our apparent shortcomings and step out in faith, and allow God to use us to equip the people we are called to serve. African American Baptist Churches desperately need viable ministries of Christian education.

Being a "natural born" African American Baptist, I am keenly sensitive to the needs of the Baptist constituents. Also, I am well aware of our powerful possibilities for growth and change. The latent realities of most of our congregations have been fertile ground for powerful, life-changing ministry. I believe that we have the potential to spark a neo-Reformation in Christian education and bring needed life into every congregation.

The model I propose may be profitably used to bring out the best in our congregations. Furthermore, the model builds upon the resident strengths of our tradition and does much to offset our apparent weaknesses. The Congregational-Enablement model is formed out of the accumulated responses and reactions of my own struggle toward trying to make "light" shine in "dark places." In this publication I am privileged to include a powerful illustration of how the enablement model should look in real life. Interestingly, the idea behind the illustration comes from outside the African American community. Nonetheless, the need for Christian education is evident throughout our beloved National Baptist Convention, USA, Inc., as well other African American church bodies. The work that follows is a humble effort to address that particular need and to assist in the process of equipping people for relevant ministry.

A final introductory remark: It is never my intention to promote simplicity at the expense of quality. I will present my ideas as clearly and as simply as possible. However, I want no one to assume the task of Christian Education to be a simple one. Christian Education within the local African American Baptist church refuses to be a simple undertaking. The educational journey of blacks on every front in America has been fraught with difficulties. I cannot speak for other Baptist bodies, but I do know that the institutional realities within the local African American

Baptist Church are replete with emotional and political complexities. Yet I firmly believe that the work of Christian education is, nonetheless, constructively challenging and richly rewarding. If meaningful benefits are to be reaped, the proposed model demands and requires responsible stewardship. What I offer is a "tried-and-tested" model, not magical solutions to a Christian dilemma.

In conclusion, I want to further assert that only committed and consistent, dedicated and deliberate efforts will bring forth the "good fruits" of Christian discipleship.

DISCUSSION QUESTIONS

1. What would a Ministry of Christian Education mean in your church?

2. What is the ultimate goal of Christian education?

3. What does Christian education provide for believers on the journey of faith?

4. What are the dynamics of "popular" religion?

5. Discuss what it means to "bluff" in the church.

6. Discuss "congregational" in the Baptist tradition.

II. Some Assumptions that Guide the Task

A Theology for Giving Power to the People

No task can be responsibly approached without some basic assumptions or driving beliefs. My understanding of assumptions is not the same as being presumptuous. Presumptuousness, as in being arrogantly certain, will undermine most tasks. My understanding of assumption has to do with possessing some basic beliefs that will drive and support the pursuit of a desired objective. The objective in this instance is developing a Ministry of Christian Education within the average Baptist church. Thus, I believe there should be some basic beliefs that support the development of a Ministry of Christian Education. I further believe that any ministry that claims to assist in the fulfillment of the "Great Commission" should be as thoughtful as possible.

I want to begin by sharing what I believe to represent some of the basic assumptions of Jesus. These assumptions are actually theological assertions that provide a way of thinking about the ministry of Christian education. I will then propose what I believe should be the basic assumptions of those who engage in the ministry of Christian education.

The Assumptions of Jesus
1. Humanity as God's Crowning Creation

We need only look to Jesus as a reference for the formulation of a theology of discipleship, or of some task assumptions. Jesus clearly entered into our world with certain fundamental assumptions about the human situation. Among his assumptions were, first of all, humanity represented the central part of creation that God felt very strongly about. According to the Bible, God felt so strongly about the creation of humanity that God imprinted us with his image and likeness. We see in the Bible humanity being portrayed as God's crowning creation. Jesus' coming in human form further testified of the glory of humanity. He did not come in any other form of creation. He came as a human being and "dwelled among us."

Jesus' acquaintance with Israel's understanding of creation, particularly as it is expressed in Psalm 8, shaped his understanding of humanity. The human being, made uniquely in the image and likeness of God, represented the focal point of God's saving work.

2. Humanity Existed In Fallen-ness

Jesus understood the true state of humanity. He had no illusions about the human condition. He knew that humanity was living below God's creative intention. Fallen-ness can very easily be described as the human tendency to live below God's creative intention and expectation. However we define "the fall," the results are always the same: humanity being less than what it was created to be. Paul Tillich, a European theologian, described fallen-ness as the human tendency toward "nonbeing", a proclivity to not be all that God created us to be. Ever since the original act of disobedience (Genesis 3), humanity has ceased to be what God intended for us to be.

> *"Jesus' coming into the world was God's ultimate response to humanity's fallen state."*

The efforts of the law and the prophets did nothing but highlight and exacerbate the condition of human fallen-ness. Jesus' coming into the world was God's ultimate response to humanity's fallen state. In a very real way the incarnation represented God's commitment to do something radical about redeeming the human condition. The preaching and teaching of Jesus exposed further the fallen-ness of humanity, but it also offered redemption. The matter of fallen-ness prompted the greatest expression of God's love. God believed, and yet believes, that humanity is redeemable.

3. Humanity Is Redeemable

The Jesus-event clearly illustrated how God ultimately feels about humanity, as well as all creation. Jesus provided a God point of view on what God will go through to redeem us. Jesus allows the world to see that God views humanity as being worth divine sacrifice. Jesus is God's incarnational "in spite of." In spite of humanity's tendency to be less than God intends, God reveals the fact that human beings can be redeemed. God demonstrates the boundlessness of His love in that "while we were yet sinners, Christ died for us" (Romans 5:8). In Jesus, God gives of God's self to bring us back to our true selves.

Jesus' involvement in the lives of persons who were considered insignificant revealed God's commitment to save to the utmost. The outcasts of society were welcomed by Jesus. The worst of the world were recipients of his care. He touched those who were considered untouchable. He counted those of inestimable worth who were not normally counted. African American Christians are certainly witnesses of the redeeming power of Jesus Christ. While the world has sought to negate us, Jesus affirmed us. While the world demeaned us, Jesus esteemed us. While the world isolated us, Jesus restored us. While the world demonized us, Jesus divinized us.

Jesus' entry into the painful ugliness of our situation was a fundamental assumption of humanity being redeemable.

4. God Loves All People

One of the most loved passages of the Bible summarizes

The Congregational Enablement-Model Revisited

the gospel's intention: "For God so loved the world that He gave his only begotten Son, that whosoever believeth in him should not perish, but have everlasting life" (John 3:16). Jesus' involvement in the redemption of all persons demonstrated God's love for all people. There is no one beyond the reach of God's love. Furthermore, the extent of God's sacrifice in Jesus' crucifixion profoundly illustrates the boundless love of God.

Paul's world-altering missionary journeys revealed the inclusiveness of God's love. The breakthrough of Christendom into the hearts of the Gentile community demonstrated that God's love was not to be confined to a Jewish sect. The claims of Christ were such that the world has come to know of God's love for all people. In fact, one Biblical writer's theology summarized God as love (1 John 4:8b). Jesus entered into the divisiveness of fallen humanity, revealing God's love for all people.

5. God Ultimately Has Power over Evil

The resurrection of Christ has registered God's power over evil. God's power over evil was demonstrated by Jesus' willingness to suffer at the hands of evil. Jesus surrendered his life into the hands of evil, but God raised him from the dead. Death, the ultimate enemy of life, was decisively defeated in Jesus Christ. Jesus' resurrection served notice of God's commitment to empower humanity to live victoriously. However evil manifests its death-dealing plan, God has power over evil.

Some Fundamental Assumptions for Christian Educators – A Theology for Christian Educators that Gives Power to the People

As Christian educators, we must also enter into our respective ministries (or tasks) with certain fundamental assumptions. There must be basic theological guideposts to direct us along the journey of Christian education. Among our most fundamental assumptions, I believe, must be the following:

1. *People Are Of Ultimate Worth*

All that we do should give testimony to the worth of people. Jesus came so that people might have life, not so that programs can live or for traditions to survive. It sometimes appears that we believe the people are for the church and not the church for the people. Such an approach to ministry is a gross misrepresentation of the Christian faith. We must fully embrace the worth of people, for it is how we view people that will determine the quality of our work. We cannot ignore Jesus' pointed assessment of how we must view people. Our active engagements in the lives of people reveal what we really feel about Him. The way we treat people demonstrates how we treat Him, particularly in our treatment of the "least of these" (Matthew 25).

All persons who endeavor to do the work of Christian education must understand that people are of ultimate worth to God; as a consequence, people are of ultimate worth to us. Whatever will happen in the life of a church will happen because people will make it happen. However successful our ministries of Christian education, it is our people who will make them successful. Thus, the work of Christian education is best approached with a high estimate of people.

2. *The Fallen State Of Humanity*

Christian educators must also understand the fallen-ness of humanity. Human disobedience to divine purpose has resulted in total alienation. All of us are in some state of fallen-ness, or predicament of alienation. Alienation means to be separated from the context of where we belong. We are not where we belong, nor are the people to whom we minister where they belong. We belong in healthy relationship with God, with others, with self, with the world, and with divine purpose. Unfortunately, all of us are alienated from some point of our divine orientation. When we are not where we belong, we have essentially fallen from our created purpose. No matter how we put it, there is nothing upward about alienation. Alienation is fallen-ness.

> *"When Christian educators approach Christian education with a healthy understanding of the fallen-ness of humanity, a redemptive level of compassion is generated."*

When Christian educators approach Christian education with a healthy understanding of the fallen-

Give Power to the People!

ness of humanity, a redemptive level of compassion is generated. Such an understanding enables us to love people, however unbecomingly they may behave. We will understand that even "saved" folk who lack understanding can behave in unregenerate ways. Moreover, we will be sensitive to our own fallen nature and not allow it to sabotage our ministry. A healthy view of our fallen state helps us to not be so easily bloated with pride, puffed in self-righteousness, or fooled by our partial learning. The church is full of fallen people, and we are numbered among the fallen.

3. Jesus Christ Provides Total Salvation for Humanity

The fallen-ness of humanity is completely addressed in Jesus Christ. Christian educators should be thoroughly convinced of the belief that Jesus saves "to the utmost." The salvific importance of Jesus should never be minimized nor compromised. Jesus saves! Moreover, there is none who is so wretched that Jesus cannot save. There are no situations beyond the saving power of Jesus Christ. Jesus saves! Jesus provides a means of healing the chasm of our fallen-ness.

The salvation wrought by Jesus reconciles the alienating forces that keep us from meaningful relations with God, others, self, the world, and divine purpose. Jesus provides a reconciling means to our full humanity. In fact, it is the saving work of Jesus Christ that shapes the goals of Christian education. We pursue the goals of Christian education because of Jesus.

Christian educators must view the saving work of Jesus Christ as an essential dynamic of Christian education. All that we do is the result of, the goal of, and the driving force of what God has provided for us in Jesus Christ. "And all things are of God, who has reconciled us to himself by Jesus Christ" (2 Corinthians 5:18a).

4. The Church Represents Jesus Christ in the World

A practical understanding of the nature and mission of the church is essential to the task of Christian education. Without getting bogged down in technical terms, such as "ecclesiology," I believe that a practical understanding of the nature and mission of the church is: the church represents Jesus Christ in the world. Jesus said, "You shall be <u>my</u> witnesses...." Whatever the church should be in the world is determined by whatever Jesus is in the world. If Jesus represents a liberating force in the world, the church should represent a liberating force. If Jesus symbolized the inauguration of God's kingdom in the world, the church should symbolize the inauguration of God's kingdom in the world. If Jesus demonstrates the willingness of God to engage in redemptive suffering, the church should demonstrate a willingness to engage in redemptive suffering. "Where two or three or gathered together in my name I am in the midst" (Matthew 18:20).

The church exists because Jesus exists. The body of Christ represents the presence, power, and purpose of Jesus Christ. Christian education is best addressed when girded by a clear understanding of the nature and mission of the church. When the church is understood as Christ's presence in the world, we avoid a lot of confusing ideas about what we ought to be doing. We do whatever Jesus did, and whatever He yet does. We make real the saving activities of God. Likewise, when the church is understood as the power of Jesus in the world, we make real the presence of One who enables the world to be what God intended. The church enables persons to experience full humanity in relationship with God, others, self, and the world. Furthermore, when the church is understood as Christ's presence in the world, we make real the fulfillment of divine purpose. The church provides the world the context in which God's will can be redemptively discerned and realized.

5. The Church Equips People to Equip Others for Faithful Service

Since the church represents Jesus in the world, one of its major tasks is to equip believers for faithful service. Jesus comes not to be served, but to serve. Jesus' calling of the disciples sets the pattern for the equipping approach to service (or ministry). Service, then, is best provided when we are adequately equipped. The more we have to work with, the better we can work. The more empowered God's people, the more we can be God's people. Christian education enables people to access more of what God has given us to work with.

Christian educators must understand that a major function of the church is to equip people for faithful service, which is to use for God what God has given us to work with. I marvel at how easily many Christians assert a belief that God will say to them, "Well done, my good and faithful servant," when they have not done anything representative of faithful service. Was not the tragedy of the one talent man a failure to use what God had given him to work with (Matthew 25:14-30)? Christian educators must enable Christians to understand that God seeks service that advances redemptive purposes by using what God has given us. In too many instances, much of what is advanced in our churches has little to do with redemption.

The task of equipping people for faithful service must be done in such a way that equipping becomes perpetual, that is, one disciple makes other disciples. The church is responsible for the ongoing equipping of its adherents. I believe that the equipping responsibility, however, is the major responsibility of Christian education.

6. *Christian Education Is The Church's Primary Equipping Ministry*

The work of Christian education is faithfully pursued when Christian education is clear about its specific assignment. The specific assignment of Christian education is to provide the church with a ministry that facilitates the disciple-making process. It is through the ministry of Christian education that persons are enabled to be "the church", or empowered to be the people God has called. Such an understanding of the task of Christian education is not limited to the activities of an organized Ministry of Christian Education.

There are a number of ministries that could conceivably assist in equipping people for service, such as Church Schools, Bible Classes, and even Youth Ministries. However,

Christian education must serve to undergird all equipping activities with a sense of cohesive purpose. In other words, everything that each ministry does should support the overall vision of the congregation. The Ministry of Christian education serves to give consistency and coherence to the other forms of ministry. Even preaching should be guided by the concern of Christian education. (This contention is expounded upon later and is illustrated in the appendices.)

The Primary Assumptions That Guide This Work

1. Christian Education Can Be a Powerful Vehicle for the Salvation and Liberation of African American People

The plight of African American people has been aptly characterized by the Scriptural notation, "My people are destroyed for a lack of knowledge" (Hosea 4:6a). Historically, African American people have been oppressed by the constant deprivation of knowledge essential to human fulfillment, and in many instances for survival. Our oppressors have always understood that it is difficult to oppress a people who "know." Thus, knowledge of who we are and where we come from, as well as Whose we are, has been historically kept away from us. One bedrock of the ugly institution of slavery was to deprive slaves of essential knowledge. It was considered a crime punishable by death to educate Black slaves. Although a few whites did teach slaves, they did it at risk of being ostracized from the slaveholding community.

A major catalyst for the abolition of slavery, the insurgence of the Civil Rights Movement, and the destruction of Apartheid, was the power of knowledge. Once people began to understand the exigencies of oppression, they were emboldened to challenge the institutions of oppression. Most of this knowledge had its beginnings in the discourses of Christian education, in spite of the oppressors' attempt to use Christianity to oppress. Slavery died because truth could not hold its peace. Civil Rights were sought because of what justice teaches. Apartheid was crushed by the overwhelming forces of well-informed righteousness and the persistence of truth. Martin Luther King, Jr.'s voice for freedom and equality was magnified by the eloquence of his intellect. All of these oppression-fighting forces have their beginnings in the knowledge wrought through Christian education.

> *"The continuing struggles of Black people can be courageously confronted with the aid of Christian education."*

The continuing struggles of Black people can be courageously confronted with the aid of Christian education. The African American church must utilize the eternal truths of knowledge to lead our people to total liberation. God's word is still, "You shall know the truth and the truth shall make you free" (John 8:32). Christian education can yet be used by God to set forth the parameters of our liberation.

2. Christian Education Provides Creative Impetus for the Obsolete Practices That Besiege Most Churches

I once received a letter from a business entity, which had this line as a part of its advertisement: "One definition of ignorance is to keep doing things the same way and expect different results." Another well-known adage, promoted as "The Seven Last Words of the Church" is: "We never done it like this before." The emphasis of both of these statements clearly aims at the troubling state of many congregations. Many of our churches are besieged with obsolescence. We are faithful to a multitude of activities that have no relevance for our current situations. So much of what occupies space on the church's program, takes up the church's time, depletes the church's energy, and dissipates the church's resources has very little to do with where people are now. We do much of what we do simply because we have always been doing it.

It must be stated that some of the resistance that often confronts those who seek change has some merit. Certainly change for the sake of change can be as futile as no change. We must be cautious of the kinds of changes we make; when we make changes; and the motives for making changes. To be sure, most of our congregations would benefit from the creative energy of some major changes.

Christian education can be an exciting vehicle for facilitating necessary changes. For one, Christian education can assist our congregations in the process of assessing their current situation. When the current needs of the congregation are placed alongside the current practices of a congregation, the need for change can become obvious to all.

Second, Christian education can be used to biblically nurture a congregation for change. Unless a congregation has reduced itself completely to a reprobate state, the Bible can soften the tough tendencies of the most stubborn of congregations.

Third, Christian education enables a congregation to see the benefits of necessary change. All changes made in the church should lead to bettering its witness for Jesus Christ. It is true that a church that is not changing is dying.

Fourth, Christian education purifies the motives for change. The motives for church changes should always transcend the mess of personalities and focus on the marvel of Christian purpose, which is making disciples. Change for the sake of change is foolish, frustrating, and a woeful waste of time.

One assumption that guides this writing is that those who have the capacity to read are persons who can assist in facilitating the redemptive changes in Black Christendom. Changes that advance the causes of redemption can only make for a more exciting and energized witness. I have personally been energized by the possibilities of Christian education providing a means of making Black Baptist churches more effective in making disciples for Jesus Christ. I am convinced that the best thing that can happen to a person, even a long-time believer, is to become a life-long disciple of Jesus Christ.

3. Every Church Possesses Disciple-Making Possibilities

Another assumption that guides this writing is the bold belief that every church has disciple-making possibilities. The very fact that a group of people gather in Jesus' name implies the potential for making disciples. The fact that people gather regularly and give of their time, as well as their resources, further implies the disciple-making possibility. We must insist that if a church has "two or three gathered in his name," discipling should be its primary business.

Too often a church has neglected its primary business by underestimating itself. We erroneously look at ourselves and make determinations about the power of God. The size of a church does not a disciple make. Disciples are made when a church has Jesus in its heart and God's love in its blood and the Holy Spirit's empowerment. The most radical thing that can happen to your church is for you to believe the following statement: Your church can make disciples!

> *"We erroneously look at ourselves and make determinations about the power of God."*

4. Every Congregation Can Become an Enablement Station

I proceed in this writing on the assumption that every congregation can become an enablement station. An enablement station is where each member can be empowered to experience life as God intends. An enablement station is a Christ-centered, Biblically-based congregation, where people are empowered to courageously face life, no matter how difficult. An enablement station is a gathering of believers who draw life-changing energy at the foot of the Cross and on the other side of an empty tomb. An enablement station is a fellowship of believers who have been seized by the presence of the Resurrected Lord and are empowered by the Holy Spirit to give witness to God's love. An enablement station is where Christians are empowered to produce fruit, but are also opened to be pruned for greater fruitfulness.

The Enablement Model of organizing a Department of Christian Education makes dynamic empowerment stations out of local congregations, because it seeks to produce dynamic disciples. Once people experience God's power in their lives, an empowerment station is realized within the context of the local church. Every local congregation can be used to enable God's people.

If you have read the book to this point, I assume you are serious about Christian education. Please read on.

QUESTIONS FOR DISCUSSION

1. Discuss the "assumptions" of Jesus. How are they relevant to Christian education?

2. Discuss the "assumptions" of Christian education.

3. Discuss the "assumptions" of this writing on Christian education.

III. Defining the Task

Clarifying the Power Given to the People

A ministry as vital as Christian education deserves clarity of role, function, and objectives. To speak of Christian Education and the Ministry of Christian Education without any definition would be a presumptuous undertaking. In most National Baptist churches, the role, function, and objectives of Christian Education remain largely unclear. Such lack of clarity results in the absence of an intentional ministry of education. We owe it to ourselves to at least give effort toward making the assignment understandable. Some clarity of the task may well help us toward fulfillment of the task.

Religious Education in the Old and New Testaments

I believe we can profit by reflecting upon the educational emphasis of the Old and New Testaments. The witness of the Bible suggests that the formation of a particular faith perspective was more valued than secular education. Perhaps it was assumed that a healthy faith perspective provided for a healthy secular perspective. A core value of Israel and the early church was the faith responses made to the revelations of God. God's revelations provided the primary curricula for religious education.

One interpretation of the creation narrative suggests education, enlightenment, consciousness or comprehension as the first order of creation. The point is that when God said, "Let there be light" (Genesis 1:3), creative comprehension preceded physical light. The creation of moon, sun, and stars--physical lights--succeeded the light of comprehension (Genesis 1:14). One might further suggest that physical lights mean nothing without mental comprehension. The suggestion is that we must understand what we are looking at before it can have any meaning. Thus, the order of creation implies that understanding, or education, is a prerequisite for participating in God's world.

The pilgrimage of the Israelites required the continuous "teaching" of God's activities to succeeding generations. "And that you may teach the children of Israel all the statutes which the Lord hath spoken unto them..." (Leviticus 10:11). Every significant development in the lives of the Israelites was added to the faith curriculum. God does not

The Congregational Enablement-Model Revisited

impinge upon the lives of a people without meaningful intentionality. God's chosen people are chosen to be taught the ways of faith. "Show me your ways O Lord, teach me your paths; guide me in your truth" (Psalm 25:4).

Another expression of Old Testament educational emphases are the wisdom writings. One can hardly read such books as the Book of Proverbs, Ecclesiastes, Songs of Solomon, Job, and Lamentations without being educationally enriched and consciously enlightened. The making-sense of the world is powerfully expressed within the Wisdom writings. The Book of Proverbs hinges on the maxim, "The fear of the Lord is the beginning of knowledge; but fools despise instruction" (Proverbs 1:7).

The prophetic writings deeply enrich our faith understanding as we seek God's justice in the world. Hosea's utterance about the tragic plight of his people had everything to do with a lapse of godly understanding (Hosea 4:6), one of which was denying the people of faith access to God's redeeming future. According to Walter Brueggemann, the prophets are those who stir up memory (teach), so as to energize the faith community into the future.[4] Any practice of religion that ignores the future misses the essence of real faith. Real faith comprehends God's acts in the past as creative impetus for the challenges of the future, as faith is lived out in the present.

In the gospels Jesus is portrayed as a teacher, "One who teaches with authority." The invitation to discipleship

---

4   Walter Brueggemann, *The Prophetic Imagination*, *(Fortress Press, Philadelphia, PA, 1978), p.13.*

Give Power to the People!

is characterized as a learning opportunity, or an educational experience. "Take my yoke upon you, and <u>learn</u> of me..."(Matthew 11:29). The Great Commission, which sums up the mission of the church, possesses an educational dimension: "Go ye therefore, and <u>teach</u> all nations... <u>teaching</u> them to observe all things whatsoever I have commanded you" (Matthew 28:19-20). The early church, as expressed in the Acts of the Apostles and the Epistles, gave serious attention to teaching. The educational ministry of the early church never separated worship from teaching. A portrait of early church worship is given in Acts 2:42: "And they continued steadfastly in the apostle's <u>doctrine</u> (teaching) and fellowship, and in the breaking of bread, and in prayers."

The teaching ministry headed the list of emphases in the early church's worship. The big task for Paul was to be assured that sound doctrine was taught to early converts. All serious adherents to the Gospel of Jesus Christ viewed teaching as essential to responsible discipleship. In fact, the word "disciple" means "student."

The concept of the university was a creation of the church. The twelfth century monastery laid the groundwork for the establishment of institutional learning, by having priests separated from the world for the purpose of study and prayer. Most of the highly esteemed universities in the world, including America's Ivy League schools, have strong religious roots. My father's generation attended school in the same buildings that housed the church. All of our historically Black colleges and universities find their origin in the race's desire to shape functional Christian men and women. Thus, the tradition of education in our culture has been nurtured in some ways by a desire to make Christian disciples.

Defining Christian Education

I trust that the above Biblical biopsy and cultural synopsis served to demonstrate the role of teaching in the Christian tradition. The Bible, as the primary source, gives credible witness to the necessity of Christian education. In the light of such a witness, I now venture to further define Christian education. Although definitions abound from other perspectives, our own struggle to define the task is needed. In embarrassing brevity, Christian education can be defined as those processes that enable us to become functional Christians. Such a definition, although limited in words, says much about the ministry of Christian education.

> *"Christian education can be defined as those processes that enable us to become functional Christians."*

Christian Education as a Process

Christian education involves a process or processes. In other words, Christian education is composed of a system of educational experiences that produces a functional Christian. The idea of "process" richly broadens the educational task. No narrow scope of educational exposure produces a wholesome Christian. The need is to incorporate a wide variety of learning experiences into our Christian pilgrimage. We live in a complex society that will not be simplified through any single point of reference or point of view. God has given us a big world, with many teachers, and multiple lessons - all for our betterment. Christian education is, therefore, a process.

As a process we see ourselves as becoming, or being. We approach the task of Christian education with the sensitivity of witnessing continuous movement, instead of the production of finished products. We are, in fact, human beings not humans done! Such an understanding means much in facilitating the church from a posture of stagnation and immobility into becoming an enablement station.

Christian Education as Enabling

Christian education involves enabling. It enables people to become Christians. It empowers people to continue the process of becoming. Christian education endeavors to supply the means, knowledge, opportunity, inspiration and motivation necessary for Christian growth. Christian education endeavors to make possible and feasible the necessities for responsible Christian nurture.

In some venues enabling is viewed as a negative. For instance, there are behavioral patterns of people in relationships with alcoholics and addicts that contribute to the addictive behavior. The understanding of enabling used in our definition is a positive, for it sees the role of the Christian as enabling others to experience the fulfilled life in Christ. One of the tasks of Christian education, therefore, is to assist people in realizing the fullness of life uniquely experienced in a relationship with Jesus and in the life of His church.

Christian Education as Becoming

Another emphasis of our definition is "to become." Christian education nurtures the notion of "becoming" a Christian. Any Christian who has already arrived is either dead or a pseudo-Christian. Christianity, properly understood, is always a "becoming", thus making necessary continuous experiences of Christian education. Whether we like it or not, we are never complete and privy to the whole counsel of God. Such foolishness bedeviled the early church, so John wrote, "Beloved, now we are sons of God, and it does not yet appear what we shall be: but we know that, when he shall appear, we shall be like him, for we shall see him as he is" (1 John 3:2). In Paul's litany of love, he reminds us that "we see through the glass dimly."

The process of becoming seeks to enable a person into being a functional Christian. A functional Christian is one who assumes the full responsibilities of discipleship. Such responsibilities include seeking ways to use one's giftedness to enhance the collective witness of the church, in the church and in the world. As we all know, too many within our congregations are not functional. Many occupy church rolls with no impacting church role. Too many of our people inconsistently attend, contribute little, and make no real impact on the quality of life within the congregation or in the world A functional Christian sees his or her whole life as an opportunity to give witness to the saving wonder of Jesus Christ.

In dialogue with Christian educators from other denominational persuasions, I noted striking similarities with the above definition. Jim Wilhoit states that "Christian education is dedicated to helping people discover God's meaning for life. It aims to enable them to gain a liberating perspective and lifestyle."[5] Eugene C. Roelhkepartian attempts to give focus to Christian education when he states, "Christian education is defined broadly as programs and events intentionally offered by a congregation to teach faith to children, teenagers, and adults."[6] Defining Christian education clearly has to do with intentional processes that enable a functional Christian.

The definition of Christian education that shall shape this presentation emphasizes it as a process, an enabling, and a becoming, with the goal of a person becoming a functional Christian. In essence, Christian education facilitates the process, enables the opportunities, and emphasizes the becoming.

It should also be noted that the concerns of Christian education revolve around the central concern of the gospel, which is human fulfillment found only within a meaningful relationship with God. The alienation of our humanity receives sin-conquering power from the gospel (Luke 4:18-19). Sin's forces keep us from experiencing life

---

5   Jim Wilhoit, <u>Christian Education: The Search for Meaning</u>, *(Baker Book House, Grand Rapids, Michigan, 1991), pp.11-12.*
6   *Eugene C. Roelhkepartain,* <u>The Teaching Church: Moving Christian Education to Center Stage</u> *(Abingdon Press, Nashville, Tennessee, 1994), p. 26.*

as God intended, but the gospel allows us to experience life and to experience it more abundantly (John 10:10b). Thus, the concern of Christian education is to bring the gospel to bear upon human lives, particularly the lives of professing Christians. It is only when the full impact of the gospel weighs heavily upon Christians that they will move from weak church membership to empowered Christian discipleship.

Three areas of the gospel that are essential to any comprehensive understanding of the concerns of Christian education are: the message (kerygma), the service (diakonia), and the fellowship (koinonia).[7] Our approach to Christian education must first seek to clarify the rich meanings of the Christian message. Second, we must transform the meaning of the message into active Christian service. (I believe many of our understandings as to what is actually Christian service need clarification.) Third, we must enhance the vitality of our fellowship. The human need for meaningful relationships ought to find it nobly expressed and fulfilled within the household of faith (Hebrews 10:24-25).

Again, the objective of Christian education is to produce a well-rounded Christian who faithfully engages in Christian discipleship. A Christian disciple is one who continues the work of Jesus and not merely worships Jesus. In fact, real worship of Jesus is to do the work of Jesus.

---

7   *The importance of a comprehensive understanding of presenting the gospel is powerfully explicated in the following publication: George Hunter, III ,The Contagious Congregation(Abingdon Press, Nashville, Tennessee, 1979). I see where the implications of Hunter's work have tremendous relevance for Christian education.*

The work of Jesus is to bring humanity into harmonious relationship with God, the world, self, and others. This task includes the bold assertion to oppose any and every power of sin. The designs of the demonic always include deception, which responsible Christian education adamantly confronts. The way to the joy of truth usually has to pass through the pain of falsehood.

Christian education has as its primary task that of perpetuating disciples, who in turn perpetuate more disciples. The perpetual discipling of humanity makes Jesus real in the world, thus making known the gospel of Jesus Christ. Christian education serves as the primary channel in the discipling process.

To bring Christian education into an intentional form within the institutional church demands a form of ministry. The form of ministry that finds usefulness for our concern is the Ministry of Christian Education. The Ministry of Christian Education may best describe our concern because the current atmosphere of our churches probably does not further support the idea of the "Department" language. Therefore, the Ministry of Christian education should serve as the structural manifestation of the task of making disciples.

The Function of the Ministry of Christian Education

The function of the Ministry of Christian Education is to guide the local congregation into vital and vibrant dimensions of Christian discipleship. A Ministry of Christian Education seeks not only to coordinate the educational pursuits of the local congregation, but it also seeks to make certain that all major tasks of the church are undergirded with solid Christian understanding.

Every activity within the local church should take place under the scrutiny of a genuine Christian perspective. Such a perspective should not be rehashed tradition, but well-thought-out Christian truths guided with Christian concerns. The theological integrity of ministry is assured through responsible Christian education. Too much of what transpires within our congregations is built upon the shifting sands of culturally related traditions, often bogged down by the baggage of irrelevance. The Ministry of Christian Education guides the church into a relevant understanding of our ongoing mission. Thus, the primary function of a Ministry of Christian Education is to assure that the church performs well her primary task -- "the making of disciples."

The Ministry of Christian Education thus functions as an enabling mechanism within the local church. It exists so that the congregation is equipped to efficiently fulfill its reason for existence. An equipped congregation can perpetuate disciples far more effectively than an equipped clergy. Moreover, the more we have equipped for ministry, the more we can equip for ministry. Our task is to enable the congregation so that she perpetually enables herself. As we move closer to a discussion on the Congregational Enablement Approach, it may be helpful for us to consider some hindrances to Christian education, as well as the marks of a disabled church.

Give Power to the People!

DISCUSSION QUESTIONS

1. How does a healthy faith perspective shape a healthy secular perspective?

2. What are your thoughts on the Bible's witness to creative comprehension?

3. Respond to the author's view of Christian education as a process, enabling, and becoming.

4. How do you see Christian education functioning in your church?

5. Discuss the three areas of a comprehensive Christian Education Ministry: kerygma (message); diakonia (service), koinonia (fellowship).

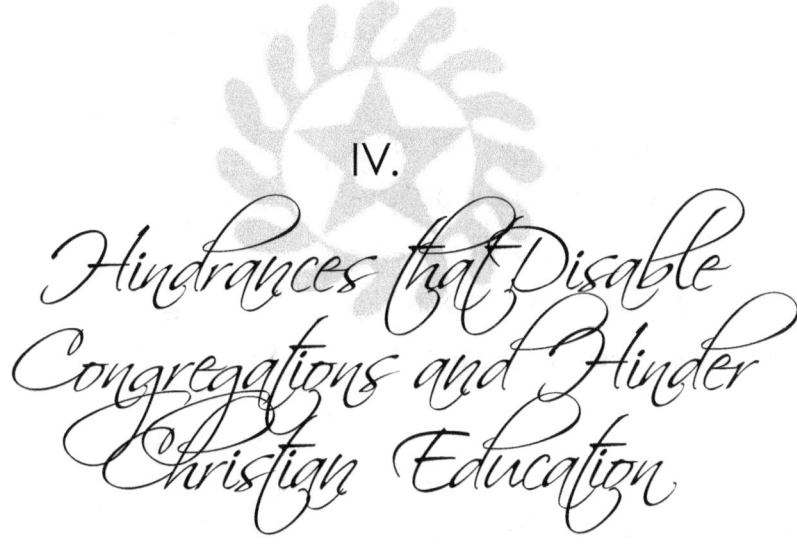

IV. Hindrances that Disable Congregations and Hinder Christian Education

Identifying Challenges to Giving Power to the People

The ministry of Christian education finds its greatest challenge directly within the culture of the local church. Not only does the Baptist denomination have a unique culture, every congregation has a unique subculture. The subculture of a congregation has to do with those conscious and unconscious realities by which a congregation organizes its life. One prime example is the gathering for worship at 11:00 a.m. on Sunday. Most congregations order congregational life around the Sunday, 11 o'clock hour. The 11 o'clock hour is held in high regard, and in most Baptist congregations nothing else is scheduled on Sunday morning at 11 o'clock. Very

Give Power to the People!

few who gather at 11 a.m. for worship, however, consider that this time was originally set to accommodate needs within an agricultural context. The cows needed to be milked and cared for in the morning, thus, making the 11 o'clock hour more amenable for the farming culture.

> *"A congregation can limit its own potential by believing in its own world-belittling consciousness with its disempowering myths."*

Many of the auxiliaries that are featured in a local congregation provide cultural verities to a congregation's life. For example: ushers in uniform, choirs in robes, Sunday School at 9:30 A.M., business meetings on a certain night, and the list goes on. However, built within the subcultures of the local church are behavioral patterns that shape congregational consciousness. Inevitably, the way our conscious is shaped determines how we perceive reality and how we give shape to our lives.

It is of interest that a congregation's life can be shaped by some generalizations that are without substance. In other words, there are some myths being perpetuated in the local church that hinder viable Christian education programs. In Paul's writing to Timothy, he argued against the church being shaped by unfounded fables and myths (1 Timothy 1:3-4). Many unfounded notions have erected barriers against empowering meaningful ministry. Therefore, a congregation can limit its own potential by believing in its own world-belittling consciousness with its disempowering myths. The problem with myths is that myths have a way of producing other myths. If a congregation is not careful, the consciousness of the church can become totally mythical.

The average Baptist church has certainly been shaped by some mythical dynamics, many of which hinder Christian education. In a rather fascinating study, five major myths were held up as common in the consciousness of congregations that resist meaningful programs of Christian education. According to the findings of the *Effective Christian Education Study,* there are some historical and social factors that have led to a number of myths in Christian education.[8] The five major myths are:

1. Christian education is for children. This myth is reflected in the higher number of children involved in Christian education programs, versus adult involvement. The problem with this myth is that it gives the disturbing message that such matters as prayer and Bible study are for children. As a result, we have an enormous number of adults walking around trying to live off a thirteen year-old understanding of the Christian Faith.

What is needed is a view of Christian education that promotes discipleship as a lifelong process. We are always at a stage in life for more mature faith formation.

2. A good Christian education program is a big Christian education program. This myth is the result of the

---

8   *Op. cit., Roehlkepartian, pp.29-33.*

Give Power to the People!

church buying into another myth, "the bigger is better mentality." This myth totally ignores the fact that the most revolutionary "Christian" education program was composed of thirteen, Jesus and the twelve. It is certainly desirous that every congregation would grow. However, not every congregation has nurtured the dynamics for numerical growth. Nevertheless, every congregation should commit itself to the growth and maturation of its people. Again, every congregation, regardless of size, has disciple-making possibilities.

3. Good teaching means transferring information. This myth is representative of the lecture-style teaching approaches evident in most churches. Most of our congregations have teachers who basically teach the way they were taught, with a one-way information-dumping style. "This myth grows out of a teacher-centered educational approach,....the teacher [has] full responsibility for making all decisions about what will be learned, how it will be learned, when it will be learned, and if it has been learned. It is teacher-directed education, leaving to the learner only the submissive role of following a teacher's instructions."[9]

Christian education must be creative enough for more than the teacher to feel empowered. Many Christians have been disabled for life at the mercy of an information-only teaching approach. Christian education must also seek ways for persons to experience the Christian faith

---

9 . Malcolm Knowles, *The Adult Learner: A Neglected Species*, 3rd ed. (Houston: Gulf Publishing, 1984), pp. 52-53.

through discovery, as well as gaining new meaning for life.

4. Teaching can occur without training. This myth is a direct outgrowth of the preceding myth. In the Black Baptist church, this myth has been perpetuated by the fact that only a few able readers existed in so many congregations for so long. As long as a person could read, no other training was required. The major flaw of this approach is that it left in the hands of the individual teachers the responsibility of finding resources and giving shape to critical subjects. This has often resulted in poor teaching, which is ultimately poor Christian education, and disastrous discipling.

Studies have shown that the more prepared the teachers, the better the teaching, and the better the program of Christian education. To dispel this myth, adequate teacher training must become available for every congregation.

5. Christian education is separate from the rest of congregational life. This myth lives on the false notion that Christian education is unrelated to whatever takes place outside of Sunday school or Bible study. Most of our auxiliaries, and tragically many pastors, do not see where Christian education will enhance their ministries. Rarely will we find a Deacon Board spending considerable time discussing matters of Christian education. When Christian education activities are scheduled, rarely do we find large representation from ministries/auxiliaries outside of

the actual Ministry of Christian Education. The results of this myth have reduced the disciple-making possibilities of most church organizations. Moreover, the members of our churches have lives that are fragmented and compartmentalized because of the failure to integrate their faith into all of life.

IV. Characteristics of a Disabled Congregation

I have discovered that most congregations know that they are not functioning as well as they believe themselves capable, but they are unable to put a finger on exactly what is hindering progress. A truth most congregations would rather not face is: Most congregations in the new millennium are functionally disabled. A functionally disabled congregation is characterized by a serious inability to sustain progressive momentum. Some congregations are more functionally disabled than others, while others have responded to their disablement better than others. In John David Webb's book _How To Change the Image of Your Church_, there are some common characteristics among disabled congregations.[10] Disabled congregations:

1. Spend a disproportionate amount of time talking about the past;
2. Have a low self-esteem, crippled by an attitude of hopelessness and/or helplessness;
3. Attempt to grow without goals or objectives;
4. Goals are set in unrealistic time frames;
5. Rarely anticipate the possible consequences of a specific course of action or program;

---
10 . John David Webb, _How To Change the Image of Your Church_,***

6. Members of the congregation have grown older;
7. The leaders are older and have served for many years;
8. Often face recurring financial problems;
9. Frequently focus inward rather than outward;
10. Normally lack a sense of urgency;
11. Often profess to be protecting the "truth" when they are most likely protecting their turf;
12. Often communicate fear of the unknown;
13. Talk about people leaving rather than being added;
14. Buildings and grounds often are in a bad state of repair;
15. Discord often marks the internal workings of the congregation;
16. Have difficulty managing visitors;
17. Are unwilling to change;
18. Often make changes at the surface level only;
19. The minister often conveys the impression that this is just another job, is visibly bored with the situation; and/or is looking forward to relocating or retiring;
20. They believe that they must remove the current minister and find a successful "superstar" to ignite a flame.

Although the above characteristics were examined primarily in predominantly white denominations, many of the same characteristics can be found in predominantly African American congregations. In fact, the characteristics may even take on an exacerbated form because of the hybrid nature of the African American

Give Power to the People!

church. In most scenarios the challenges of the primary culture are usually exacerbated within the subcultures.

Christian education represents the only form of ministry where the above characteristics can be constructively approached and effectively eliminated. As a ministry of enablement, Christian education seeks to move congregations from postures of disablement to powers of enablement. The powers of enablement are the results of a Christian education program that sets forth principles for enablement. Webb sets forth seven principles of the enabled congregation,[11] which I want to attempt to reinterpret for African American church understanding. The Principles of an Enabled Congregation are:

Principle 1

Webb states that "enabled congregations manifest symbols, symbol systems, and stories which coincide with the individual symbols, symbol systems, and stories of a majority of their potential population."

> *"In most scenarios the challenges of the primary culture are usually exacerbated within the subcultures."*

From a Black church perspective, this has to do with a congregation's life coinciding with the life of its potential members. For example, the forties were marked with the tremendous migration movement by rural Blacks to the inner city. (The migrating Blacks created a new story for

---

11   . Ibid., pp.***

Blacks in America.) Migrating Blacks often discovered religious life (a symbol) in the city quite challenging, and sometimes unfriendly, to their rural upbringing. In response to the alienating effects of urban Black churches, rural Blacks organized churches (a coinciding story) that reflected many of the rural expressions of African American worship (a symbol). Yet, as the rural Blacks became more accustomed to urban life, the practices of the church evolved as the individuals and families evolved.

> *"New symbols will have to be created that will connect urban-born, upwardly mobile Blacks to the symbols of their rural fore-parents."*

Currently, many Black churches are shaping new symbols and stories to coincide with a generation of African Americans who have a different story. New symbols will have to be created that will connect urban-born, upwardly mobile Blacks to the symbol meanings of their rural fore-parents. There will also have to be an effort to understand the symbols and stories of the hip-hop generation. The rising popularity of Christian hip-hop cannot be ignored as irrelevant, or irreverent, to the Christian witness. Many of the Christian hip-hoppers have incredible stories of the power of God that could do much to empower the church. It would be a serious mistake to allow the dominant culture to capitalize on the relevant witness of our young people.

Principle 2

An enabled congregation has a clearly defined mission statement and clearly established goals, from which the level of accomplishment can be measured. This principle allows a congregation's life to be guided by a shared sense of mission, which has been clearly defined and articulated. The congregation's sense of mission is pursued by goals that are measurable and are clearly understood by the congregation-at-large.

This may well be one of the greatest challenges to a traditional African American Baptist congregation. The tendency to operate in response to situations, calendared activities, and often blatant impulse sabotages efforts to have a collective mission. The need for the congregation to shape ministry guided by a clearly defined mission would do much to unify and empower the disjointed and disempowering practices of many congregations. I have witnessed congregations ignore clearly defined mission statements in order to maintain the safety of established tradition. Likewise I have witnessed one of the fastest growing congregations within the African American Baptist community maintain momentum with constant reminders concerning the mission of that congregation. This congregation seems to understand that fulfilling a mission requires risk and an enabled congregation that rises to the challenge to fulfill its goals.

Principle 3

An enabled congregation communicates the message that widely distributes power and opportunity.

The Congregational Enablement-Model Revisited

This principle allows for the entire congregation to share in the creation and the fulfillment of the congregation's goals. An enabled congregation is one where every member of a congregation, or a noted majority, claim ownership in the church's mission.

In the Black Baptist church community this principle will challenge the autocratic tendencies of many pastors. Too many Black pastors have not evolved from the tribal chieftain motif that characterized the plantation church. A serious messianic complex hinders many from sharing power and distributing the responsibilities of ministry, some of which may require therapeutic intervention. It would do us well to note that not even Jesus tried to do ministry alone.

Principle 4

An enabled congregation maintains open and decentralized communication. Much could be said about the empowering energy of open communication, but suffice it to say that Pastor and people receive power when communication is not booby-trapped with cumbersome bureaucracy. When Pastor and people are in tune, with a common vision, ministry becomes a beautiful experience. It has been mine to experience the frustration of a congregation when the vision of the church is stored up in the heads of a few people, while the majority stumbles in a maze of miscommunicated ideas. We can never do enough to keep open and decentralized the essential information of the church.

Principle 5

An enabled congregation will use "integrative problem solving," in which the problems of the congregation are placed in the hands of those most likely to understand them and most committed to their solution. Although some people are naturally gifted with the peace-making gift, others can be trained to deal effectively with conflict. Currently there are many resources and agencies well-equipped to assist the church in effective conflict resolution. We are certainly encouraged by Jesus' words, "Blessed are the peacemakers, for they shall be called children of God."

Principle 6

An enabled congregation allows "challenge" in an atmosphere of trust. One of the most powerful witnesses that a congregation can give is to allow challenge to enrich its fellowship. Too often challenge is perceived as disruptive rather than constructive. The need to experience trust and be trusted does much to the human spirit. This principle welcomes differences of opinions as being helpful in giving shape to creative approaches to ministry.

This principle could function well to alleviate the pervasive distrust within the African American community. The legacy of slavery that was upheld by sowing seeds of distrust within the slave community has strong roots and much ill-begotten fruit. Unfortunately, this spirit of distrust has found fertile ground within the Black church. I have been at a loss at the many ways in which Black Christians express a lack of trust among people who are supposed to be living within a context of trust. An intentional ministry of Christian education would do much to enable a congregation to recover a spirit of trust.

Stephen Covey cites well that where there is a lack of trust progress is slow and costs are high. Likewise, where trust is high things move efficiently and with less cost.[12]

Principle 7

An enabled congregation provides appropriate awards and recognition as a means of encouraging better performance and more responsibility on the part of the total membership. Five incredible words of encouragement are: You are making a difference. How we make people feel that they are making a difference is critical to the success of ministry. Church work can often be some of the most thankless and unappreciated work in a person's life. For that cause the workload of the average church rests primarily upon the shoulders of a few. This principle draws from the Biblical admonitions to give "honor where honor is due" and "to exhort (or encourage) one another." The Christian faith, as depicted in the Bible, recognizes that everyone needs to be recognized and encouraged.

One of the traditional practices of the Black church has been to celebrate life within the congregation with Annual Days. Although this tradition has been diluted with empty

---

12   Covey, Stephen, *The Speed of Trust: The One Thing that Changes Everything*, Free Press, New York, New York, 2006.

Give Power to the People!

rituals and irrelevant ceremonies, the original intention was to acknowledge and reward. The Black church would do well to recover this much needed practice to esteem those who labor among us.

> *"How we approach Christian education will largely determine whether congregations are disabled or enabled."*

How we approach Christian education will largely determine whether congregations are disabled or enabled. I want to propose a model of developing a Ministry of Christian Education that will enable. As suggested, I refer to it as the "Enablement Model."

The Congregational Enablement-Model Revisited

QUESTIONS FOR DISCUSSION

1. What are some of the hindrances to the Ministry of Christian Education?

2. Discuss the characteristics of a "disabled" congregation.

3. Discuss the principles of an "enabled" congregation.

Give Power to the People!

V. The Congregation-Enablement Model

A Model that Gives Power to the People

The Congregational-Enablement Model is an attempt to draw from the neglected strength of the average congregation, that is, the congregation itself. Christian education in the past has often perceived the congregation as an object, rather than "the subject." As an object, the congregation is something being done unto, often with no regard for the people involved. Conversely, when the congregation is viewed as subject it is the one doing, an entity empowered to enhance the lives of people.

Too often we've brought the well-packaged goods of a select few and tried to import those goods into the life of the masses. Such an approach may work well in the marketplace of things, but it rarely works within the marketplace of ideas and faith development. If the congregation is to move, it must experience within itself, or feel within itself, the power to move.

Many past approaches to Christian education have done little to move the average congregation. In fact, some of the efforts of the past have even alienated many within the congregation. Many of our people are not a part of our educational ministries because they haven't been made to feel a part. As a result, many perceive the educational ministry to be for people other than themselves.

The time has come for us to responsibly recognize that our congregations are more than audiences, gullible to the suggestions of an elite few. Our congregations are the very forces that will enable the church to be the church. To not involve the congregation in the total educational ministry is to ultimately alienate the membership from the church's ministry. Such an act of alienation on the part of the church can be viewed as an act of blatant blasphemy against the Holy Spirit.

Another alienating effect of our past approaches is that of categorizing intelligence. Sad it is that we have perpetuated the worldly notion of "smart people" and "dumb people," or the intelligent and the ignorant. Within the African American community this was the division perpetuated by the oppressor with the distinctions made between field servants and house servants. The painful practices of coloration within the African American community also served to alienate people from one another, based upon the varied skin tones of the people. Many within the African American community viewed people of lighter hue to be more intelligent, or worthy of intelligence, because they were closer to being "white." The early church broke down the barriers of wise and foolish (Romans 1), as well as the privileges of race (Galatians 3:26-29). We, too, must understand that in Christ all are one and distinctions are invalid.

To allow so-called "smart folk" to control the activities of Christian education is to build afresh the walls of alienation, many of which are supported by a legacy of oppression. Such alienation hinders any effort at education and irreparably harms the mission of the church, especially the mission of the Black church. I have witnessed some so-called smart people be used as instruments of the Devil. They were so smart that no one understood what they were talking about. As a result, they were used as lightning rods for congregational confusion. The Congregational-Enablement Model struggles to eliminate all barriers of alienation because of the belief that we are one in Christ.

It may be that the use of the term Congregational-Enablement carries with it a note of strangeness. Interestingly, the enablement of the congregation is an inextricable part of the church's life and thought. The Holy Spirit, rightfully understood, enables the church to

Give Power to the People!

continue the ministry of Jesus Christ. Leander Keck has defined the Holy Spirit as God acting in power in the lives of His people.[13] The experience on the day of Pentecost was God acting in power in the lives of His people. In fact, the very promise of the Holy Spirit was as an enabling agent of God (Acts 1:8). In the text it says, "You shall receive power." The word for power is "dunamis," the act of being enabled, or empowered. The Congregational-Enablement model draws from the original experience of the early church and can find powerful expression in today's world.

The Congregational-Enablement Model is clearly based on the assumption that an empowered laity best expresses the church of Jesus Christ. People doing ministry more accurately embodies the intention of the New Testament church. I know that this idea may not find fertile soil with autocratic clergy persons, but the Christian church is most the church when lay people are empowered to be the church. I know of one pastor-preacher who has warned us of the danger of the word "ministry" being applied to anything other than the preacher. The church of Jesus was never intended to be a clergy movement, but a people movement, a movement

"The Holy Spirit, rightfully understood, enables the church to continue the ministry of Jesus Christ".

---

13   . Leander Keck, <u>Mandate to Witness</u>, (Judson Press, Valley Forge, PA, 1964), p. 46.

of the "laos." The Congregational-Enablement approach can be defined as that model which draws from the latent, or near latent, energies of the people, in order that the people may experience and enable one another in the fulfilling of the ministry of the church.

> *"The church of Jesus was never intended to be a clergy movement, but a people movement, a movement of the "laos.""*

A powerful illustration of what the enablement model looks like was provided to me through a book written by two pastors of the United Kingdom. Mike Breen and Walt Kallestad[14] illustrated a perception of discipleship that gives incredible credence to the enablement model, although they never used the term. Using the biblical understanding of time "kairos" as opposed to "chronos", they provided a vivid illustration how an enabled disciple works.

Chronos is the perception of time as being linear, successive, and sequential. When one views life through the "chronos" perception, he or she sees a disciple as one being saved and successively moving on toward heaven. There are no additional defining moments in life. Salvation and heaven are the hallmarks, and there is nothing of great significance in between being saved and getting to heaven. Life is a straight line of succession. Many within our churches live as though the Christian

---

14   Breen, Mike and Kallenstadt, Walt, *The Passionate Church*, Cook Communications Ministries, *Colorado, Paris, Ontario*, 2005.

experience is merely a straight line to glory, with nothing in between. As a result, too many within our congregations miss moments to participate in significant discipleship opportunities. (See illustration below)

"Kairos", however, is the perception of time where events and experiences provide opportunities to experience life in new and fresh ways. Breen and Kallenstadt called the "kairos" moments "God-given opportunities to enter into a process of learning kingdom living."[15] The Bible's understanding of time is much richer and far more comprehensive than the "chronos" perception. The Greek language, as well as the Hebrew language, viewed time with a more dramatic, comprehensive, and fulfilling understanding than a succession of events. The idea of the "fullness of time" is "kairotic", where something of great significance impacts human experience.

---

15   Ibid.,p.41.

The Congregational Enablement-Model Revisited

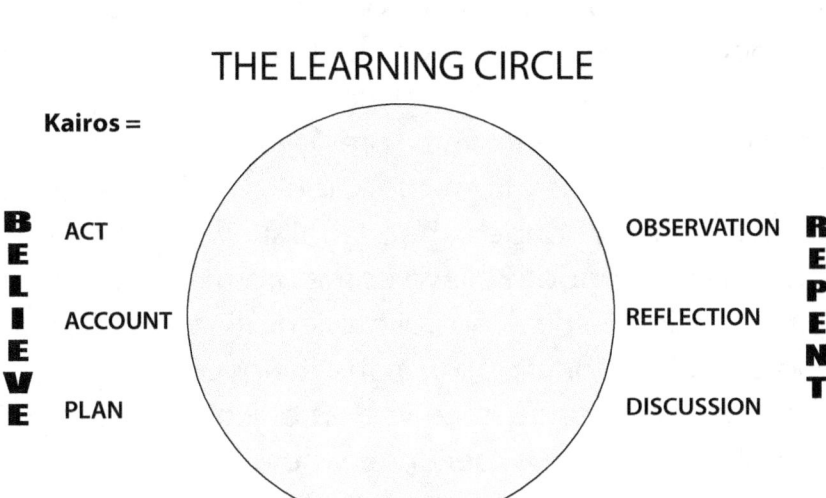

The illustration above, which Breen and Kallendstadt refer to as the "Learning Circle," provides a picture of how the enablement process works. The experience of salvation as an event that leads us to heaven is illustrated in the straight line. This represents the "chronos" perception, which is commonly held among most believers. Such an understanding is really expressed in the "once-saved-always-saved" position. Salvation is portrayed as a static procession into heaven with no regard for discipleship moments. However, the "kairos" circle seems to represent more of what Jesus referred to in Mark 1:15. Jesus began his ministry by preaching, "The time is fulfilled, and the kingdom of God is at hand. Repent and believe in the gospel."

The operative words are "time", "repent," and "believe." The notion of time being referred to is "kairos," a moment of fulfillment, or a pregnant moment. Again,

Breen and Kallestadt referred to "kairos" moments when we are allowed God-given opportunities to enter into a process of learning kingdom living. Also, salvation involves two indispensible dynamics that complement the "kairotic" moment, which are "repent" and "believe". Repentance comes from the Greek word "metanoia", which means a change of heart that shows up in a lifestyle or behavior change. Believe comes from the Greek word "pistis", which refers to a faith orientation that leads to wholehearted participation in the things of God.

When repentance is viewed as a "kairotic" dynamic, it should lead to an experience where we must observe. We must spend some time considering where we are and what has brought us to the particular "kairotic" moment. Kairotic moments can be either good, bad, or indifferent, but they have the power to change our lives dramatically. Once one observes the experience, it should lead to a time of reflection. The reflection time allows us an opportunity to probe, to ask the serious questions that lead to and support change. Why are you reacting the way you are? What were the feelings involved in the moment? Why did we feel the way we did? What emotions were brought to surface?

After serious personal reflection, it is wise to invite another into the experience through discussion. "If observing and reflecting are to lead to lasting change, we must invite others into the process. For repentance to have taken hold, we've got to share it with someone else."[16] All Christians should have at least one person

---

16   Ibid., p. 44.

The Congregational Enablement-Model Revisited

with whom they can share the learning moments of the Christian faith. Keep in mind, not all "kairotic" moments are immediately joyful. If we take seriously the Cross, many of the most profound opportunities for significant Christian growth come through suffering and shame. The joy comes after the suffering, and if we can share the suffering, the shared joy is more complete.

On the "belief" side of the Learning Circle, we note how out of the discussion we move to a plan. A plan must be made if the change we claim to have experienced in repentance is to lead to radical inner change. We have to be convinced that the issue that brought us to the "kairos" moment directed us to a place that causes us to seek more passionately God's kingdom. We must desire God's kingdom no matter the cost, or the issue with which we struggle.

As a consequence, our plan leads to a desire to be accountable. By being accountable we externalize what has been going on internally. We ask others to hold us accountable. Many people resist bringing others into certain experiences of their lives. "Being afraid to share with someone else because you think your thoughts are too private will keep you from growing and changing."[17] We cannot be Christian by ourselves. If Jesus sent them out two by two, we, too, must see our Christian experience as one which can only be authenticated through community.

The next move is to act upon what has been planned and what is being held accountable to. Our actions

---

17   Ibid. p. 50.

are expressions of faith, for faith is always expressed in the world. James said, "Faith without works is dead." It could also be said that "faith without action is dead." The Learning Circle illustrates how moments within the Christian experience provide opportunities to become a more faithful disciple. It also suggests that such moments are ongoing and can be shared with others within the process of becoming a disciple of Jesus Christ. Our experiences, when processed correctly, can be powerful tools for evangelizing and discipling others.

Most of us were brought up with some exposure to the "Slinky" toy, a series of wire circles connected into one. Instead of a straight, static line into glory, we should have a "Slinky" type journey filled with passionate and dynamic moments where we engage in the process of becoming a complete disciple. "Each time around the circle means you have grown a little more and taken on a little more of the character of Christ."[18]

The Congregational-Enablement Model also understands the Holy Spirit as "dunamin," God's power empowering the congregation with the ability to engage in responsible discipleship. This approach places the bulk of educational responsibilities into the hands of the people, making the people own the responsibility for their own faith development. Every member of the congregation can become a responsible disciple and can conceivably participate in the disciple-making process. Clergy persons facilitate faith development, while lay people engage in faith development. The congregation, therefore, engages in the process of enabling itself.

---

18   Ibid. p. 53.

The Congregational Enablement-Model Revisited

Suppose the congregation has been influenced by the arbitrary and unbiblical notions of a un-discipled Deacons' board. Out of respect for traditionalism, many within such a congregation have waited upon the halting initiatives of Deacons to shape its direction. So often the congregation-at-large perceives well the inadequacies of un-discipled Deacons, but does little to call the Deacons to a greater sense of accountability. As a result, the strong hand of tradition and the misguided notion of peace-at-all-cost keep the people from challenging leadership inadequacies. What a congregation does, in fact, is to perpetuate its own spiritual impotency. A un-discipled, un-empowered leadership can only produce its kind -- an undisciplined and disempowered congregation.

The task for such a disempowered situation is to demand a systematic and evaluated course of Christian education activities in the area of total discipleship. The Learning Circle could be used as a powerful tool in helping leaders see themselves, which can be revelatory and transformative. In a previous ministry I was led to equip our leadership in a teaching ministry called S.O.S, Seminary on Saturday. We developed systematic studies on Bible, Theology, Church History, and Leadership training on Saturday mornings at 7:30 a.m. The prospective Deacons understood the

> *"A un-discipled, un-empowered leadership can only produce its kind – an undisciplined and disempowered congregation."*

Give Power to the People!

seriousness of the matter by the sacrifice required to serve. It took sacrifice to get up early on Saturdays, and it takes sacrifice to responsibly lead the church. The fruit of such sacrifice empowers lay leadership to lead with a sense of being connected with the universal thrust of the Christian community, rather than leading from the narrow perspective of a localized tradition.

A leader who knows little about Jesus can do very little for Jesus. Likewise, one who knows nothing about Jesus, the church, and mission can hardly contribute to the work of Jesus, the work of the church, and the mission of the church. To maintain such an enfeebled, dull-witted leadership is to guarantee pastor and people continued frustrations. Such leaders can either be developed or replaced. Nevertheless, the congregation that understands itself as God's instrument of enablement never settles for un-discipled leadership.

The process of the Congregational-Enablement Model also aligns itself with the deep needs of the congregation. The thrust of this approach is not limited to leadership concerns alone. This approach to Christian education has the freedom and potential to expand into all areas of life. To set in process the steps toward giving wholeness to the life of a particular people is the ultimate objective of the Congregational-Enablement Model. Our people are empowered when they can view evidence and progress in their own struggle toward spiritual health and wholeness. People need to witness the power of Christ being manifested through them. Moreover, the Congregational-Enablement Model offers the people a chance to interpret all of life in the marvelous light of the gospel. They become the interpreters rather than the interpreted. As a result, the congregation truly becomes co-laborers with God.

An apparent strength of this approach is that the congregation begins to see itself differently. A radical self-perception energizes the effort of this approach. As a congregation views itself as having authentic power, which is not contingent upon any of the world's false senses of power, it is liberated from the awful sense of powerlessness that hinders effective ministry. A congregation's self-worth is then heightened, freeing it from petty in-house power plays and reactions to external social fluctuations. Such a congregation is now perceived as a liberating change agent, letting nothing prevent it from the spread of the gospel through its well-designed ministry objectives. The congregation is authentically empowered for mission when it has an empowered self-understanding.

An additional strength to this approach is that it enhances the congregation for worship. Powerful and celebrative worship still represents a vital feature of an empowered church. The gathering of an empowered congregation energizes worship with a celebrative spirit. People not only "shout," but they know better what they are shouting about. To be knowledgeably used of God, as an empowered disciple of Christ, offers vital energies for meaningful and celebrative worship. Every aspect of the worship can be more widely appreciated when its meanings are more widely understood. The choir that is intellectually in touch with the theological tenets of the

Faith can more powerfully and effectively give genuine praise. The people who have a grasp for the truths of Christian witness can more fervently give a witness of the Risen Lord in their midst. The preacher who has entered into the "life of the mind" can better share what God has shared. The Congregational-Enablement Model offers the Christian education stimulant for creative and celebrative worship.

Other strengths can possibly be gleaned and highlighted, but there is definitely an apparent weakness. How can a congregation be educationally enabled without some sense of direction? This model is aware of the dangers of mass confusion. Direction is a necessity for any mass effort. It is to the addressing of this challenge that we shall now turn the discussion. The Director/Minister of Christian Education represents the congregational vessel for guiding the Ministry of Christian Education.

QUESTIONS FOR DISCUSSION

1. What are some of the practices and/or behaviors that alienate people from Christian education?

2. What is the difference between "chronos" and "kairos"?

3. According to the "Learning Circle," what are the primary functions of discipleship?

4. How does the Holy Spirit function in the Ministry of Christian education?

5. Discuss the strengths and weaknesses of the Congregational-Enablement Model.

Give Power to the People!

VI. Direction for the Congregational Enablement Model

Shaping a Person who Gives Power to the People

God did not lead Israel through the wilderness without direction. A human agent was the primary source of direction, consequently creating the need for other human agents. Jesus did not engage in ministry alone. He rallied around himself other human agents who would in turn reproduce like channels of direction. As Jethro advised Moses, and as Jesus suggested to the disciples: select from among the people persons who are capable of assisting. I once heard the Reverend Jesse Jackson state, "The reason God gives us leaders is because we need them." It is advisable and practical that the pastor, with sensitive others, select from the congregation a promising individual, who will serve as the Director/Coordinator of Christian Education. The selection of a Director/Coordinator is not a contradiction in the Congregational-Enablement Model. In fact, it is a further expression of the approach.

It must be clearly understood and accepted that not any kind of director will do. The Director/Coordinator must certainly give evidence of having within him/her the "mind which was in Christ Jesus." The Director/Coordinator must show signs of the personality of Jesus Christ. A convincing Christian is a necessity, someone who possesses a personal relationship with God. The Director/Coordinator must also be a congregational person. A genuine relatedness to the masses is essential for the congregational task. He or she must be a lover of all people who can be loved by all people. Such a person is not perfect, just personable. One should understand the Christian thrust of love, which seeks to "be all things for all persons." This individual must also be sensitive to individual needs, as well as the needs of the congregation. In essence, the Director is a lover of Christ, the church, the pastor, and the people.

The Director who loves the church is one who is authentically in the love with the Lord of the Church. An authentic love for Jesus is obvious in how one relates to the people Jesus loves. No Director can honestly love the church as an institution and hold in disdain the people within the institution. Thus, it is critical that the Director/Coordinator, or Minister of Education demonstrate an authentic love for the church and its people. One measurement of a person's love for the church is how do the people relate to him or her? I always consider children as the the most accurate relational barometer of a person's authenticity. If the children demonstrate love toward an individual it is normally authentic.

The Director who loves the pastor is critical to the work of Christian education. Anyone who serves is such a critical role of Christian development must demonstrate an authentic love for the pastor. The Pastor must feel the love, know the love, and can testify of the love the person has for him or her. To place leadership in the hands of someone who does not authentically love the pastor will be a continuous drama of contention. I unreservedly suggest that the best person to testify of the love someone has for the pastor is the pastor.

Again, I emphasize that the Director must have an authentic love for the people because doing the work of Christian is a labor of love. There will be so much that the Director will encounter in providing an effective Ministry of Christian education that can only be handled with a loving heart. Since the discipleship sins of the church are many, it is necessary for love to cover the multitude of sins.

The Director/Coordinator is also an investigator--he or she believes in the task of investigating the deep truths of the gospel. He or she must possess a strong and studious belief in the magnificent rewards of Christian education. My sainted mentors referred to this as "love of the mind". The Director/Coordinator must be open-minded to the adventurous task that lies ahead. I do not believe that

College degrees should be a mandatory prerequisite for being Director/Coordinator of Christian Education, although such a person should be appreciated and preferred. Many of our churches are not yet blessed to have degreed persons throughout the congregation. Currently, the cost of education has become prohibitive, as a result hindering many from receiving a college education. Yet, the Christian Education Director/Coordinator must be independently inclined toward rigorous study. He or she must truly know of the refreshing streams found only in the studying tasks and have the initiative to engage in a journey of self-study.

One of the primary reasons the "chosen" Director must possess a strong proclivity toward studying is that he or she must engage in a thoughtful and meditative pilgrimage on the various paths trod upon in Christian education. If the Director has not received formal training in the area of Christian education, he or she must engage in a rather extensive exploratory study on what has been said, as well as who has said something, about Christian education.

I can recall my initial journey into the Ministry of Christian education. Although a seminary student, Christian education was not my focus of study. When asked to lead the Ministry of Christian Education, I spent long hours in the library, gleaning books, poring over journals, and running after references. I was driven by the belief that I had to acquaint myself with the task if I was to responsibly do the task. This experience allowed me to familiarize myself with the various nuances of Christian education. I was, therefore, able to approach the task with a greater sense of empowerment.

This study adventure will not only solidify and enrich the Director's/Coordinator's own perspective, but he or she will also be able to discern what is common and essential to most views of Christian education. Most importantly, he or she will be able to responsibly sense what is most relevant to the needs of his or her own congregation. In addition, through rigorous study, the director will gain the authoritative posture needed to coordinate the educational activities of his or her particular congregation.

The Director/Coordinator is also an educational informer. He or she is a resource person who knows and seeks the needed information. One step in developing a Department of Christian Education is to allow the Director/Coordinator a period of thoughtful study. It may not be a bad idea for the Pastor to insist that the Director/Coordinator be allowed time for initiation study. Currently, the internet provides numerous connections to accredited institutions that can enhance the preparation process. The Director/Coordinator should be allowed sufficient time to explore the many written and unwritten ramifications of Christian education. He or she must be mindful to not limit him or herself to just Baptist perspectives, but to boldly venture into the areas of other denominational views.

I was greatly enriched to discover that Christian education in American was actually a Presbyterian initiative. Originally it was the Presbyterians who emphasized structured education ministries within the church. So who did I focus upon as a primary source for understanding Christian education? If you guessed the Presbyterians, you are right. We all know only in part! The Director/Coordinator must be careful to not extract only weighty theoretical formulations, but also to expose oneself to organizational and practical concerns. The impact of solemn hours of reflective thinking will have much to do with the length, height, and breadth of the Christian education task. Thus, the task of the educational informer is to be approached with great respect. It takes an empowered person to empower people.

The Director/Coordinator is also an Enabler. He or she, as a congregational person, must embody the Congregational-Enablement Model. His or her every interaction among the people should be an expression of enabling. The Director is not just interested in doing a job; he or she endeavors to equip others to do their job better. A person who is not inflated with positions and deluded with a sense of importance best fulfills this role. An enabler never intimidates; he or she only motivates. He or she believes in the innate potential of every living person. An enabler perceives the educational process not as imparting information, but as a resource for enablement. The Director's disposition about the Christian enterprise visibly translates the enablement approach.

The enablement spirit of the Director has far-reaching influence in the organization of a Ministry of Christian Education. One of the major tasks in giving direction to a program of Christian education is to organize. It is to the task of organization that we now turn for discussion.

QUESTIONS FOR DISCUSSION

1. What are the "desired" characteristics of a Director/Coordinator of Christian education?

2. What are the "tasks" required for a Director/Coordinator of Christian education?

3. What should be some of the necessary steps in preparation to direct/coordinate the Ministry of Christian education?

Give Power to the People!

VII. Organization

The Plan for Giving Power to the People

"To fail to plan is to plan to fail."

The above words, from an unknown source, poetically give credence to the grave significance of planning. Planning is essential to an effective ministry of Christian education; more so is it essential to the Congregational-Enablement Model. The Director/Coordinator is to approach the planning stage only after a period of intensive investigation. Out of the period of investigation some vision of Christian education, relative to the particulars of one's context, should emerge. A sense of vision breaks forth and allows the Director to craft a relevant approach to the ministry. Vision is the capacity to see what God wants done where you are serving with the people with whom you serve.

Appendix A provides a simplified flow chart of how a Baptist church should look organizationally. Please note that the chart consists of some of the contemporary church organizational arrangements and ministry terms. This provides the Director/Coordinator, as well as the congregation, a perspective by which to view the church. The chart is basically suggestive, which means it is a mere tool to guide you in considering how your congregation might be ordered. The Director/Coordinator of Christian Education profits from having a broad view of the church's organizational dynamics.

In Appendix B a suggested Concept Thrust/Mission Statement is offered as a tool to guide the educational focus.

The Concept Thrust/Mission Statement

A conceptual thrust is merely stating in words the primary objectives that a ministry of Christian education, for a particular congregation, seeks to achieve. George Barna is quite helpful when he states, "A mission statement is a general statement about who you wish to reach and what the church hopes to accomplish."[19] The conceptual thrust is synonymous with a mission statement and does serve to define the mission of Christian education. (See

---

19 Barna, George, The Power of Vision (Regal Books, 2003), p. 35.

Appendix B.) The conceptual thrust/mission statement is a tool used to pave the way for the educational ministry. This tool will be most helpful when the program is introduced to the congregation.

The conceptual thrust need be no more than three paragraphs long, yet it should be stated in clear and concise language. It should be general enough so as not to intimidate the congregation, but specific enough to gain their attention and rally their support. Enough specifics should be suggested in the concept so as to clarify the task. It is imperative that the concept of Christian education for <u>your</u> church be amenable to and clearly understood by all.

Again, one must keep in mind that the concept of Christian education should always be formulated to address one's particular congregation. The uniqueness of every congregation serves as the primary guide that will move Christian education from theory to practice. Congregational uniqueness, however, does not mean cultism. Our concern is still for <u>Christian</u> education, not cultic indoctrination. There are some congregations so indoctrinated into the idiosyncrasies of the leader that it's hard to discern what is authentically Christian. To facilitate meeting the needs of each congregation, I suggest that every conceptual thrust/mission statement of Christian education should include the following components:

1. A concern for the experiences of God, as told by the Biblical witnesses. This is commonly known as Bible Study.

2. A concern for the experiences of God, as experienced within one's particular denomination, community, and congregation. This is commonly known as theology.

3. A concern for the day-to-day struggles that impact the lives of the people. The family, jobs, politics, economics, sex, drugs: these are all very real issues for the human family.

4. A concern for engaging one's Christian experiences into fulfilling the mandate of the church - "making disciples." (Evangelism is always a by-product of a good program of Christian education.)

Allow me to share a word of warning as it relates to the conceptual thrust/mission statement. To maintain its congregational sensitivities, the Director/Coordinator should never allow his or her well-thought-out concept to become the law. The conceptual thrust/mission statement serves as an orientation tool to be used to give the congregation some general ideas about the focus of the Christian education program. We must forever remain open to modify the Christian education focus to address the ever changing needs of the congregation. It is always possible that congregational needs will vary from time to time. Therefore, Director/Coordinator and concept sensitivities must always be functional and amenable to change.

The Congregational Enablement-Model Revisited

Introduction to the Congregation

The second step in organizing for Christian education involves congregational introduction. The program of Christian Education must now be introduced to the people who will make it work. There are several ways in which one can introduce the program. (See Appendix C for suggestions on the Introduction of Christian Education.) The following are a few approaches that have been used with a measure of success:

The Christian Education Planning Workshop

A Christian Education Planning Workshop is a very effective way of introducing Christian education. To facilitate such a workshop is quite simple. The Director/Coordinator should contact all church leaders: Presidents of Auxiliaries/Ministry Leaders, Sunday School Superintendent(s), Nurture or B.T.U. Director(s), Youth Leaders, Deacons, Trustees, Associate Ministers, and influential young people. The Pastor is definitely to be a part of this gathering. To exclude the pastor is to invite inevitable and destructive shortcomings, if not total failure.

The Christian Education Planning Workshop should be on a day when at least four hours can be sacrificed in complete dedication to the ministry of Christian Education. All persons contacted should be informed of the meeting and encouraged to give their wholehearted participation. The meeting should be well structured, with a printed agenda available to all. (See Appendix B.) So as to give it a note of celebration, devotional messages and praise singing are encouraged. Refreshments, during break periods, are always helpful stimulants. As the Director/Coordinator unfolds the blessings of Christian education, some visual aids may prove quite helpful. The PowerPoint presentation, along with hand-outs, represents a very powerful and creative approach.

The conceptual thrust/mission statement, a working definition of Christian education, Biblical support, and other stimulating aids should be available to enhance the effort. Providing people with comprehensive aids instills a sense of self-worth and facilitates educational objectives. The work of empowering people begins with the introduction. The meeting must move objectively, but the subjects (the congregation) must be always a part of the movement. A "regular" business meeting approach will certainly discourage participation.

It might also prove helpful to have this meeting hosted away from the church's normal gathering place. It has been proven that a neutral place has a tendency to liberate creativity. The creative impetus of the congregation's leadership is an invaluable commodity.

The Christian Education Retreat

A retreat on Christian Education is another empowering alternative. The retreat setting, away from the usual confines of the church building, offers fertile stimulation for approaching relevant Christian ministry. We should note that even Jesus pulled away from the normal traffic of life. Interestingly, Jesus often referred to children as being more receptive to the things of God. Being away

The Congregational Enablement-Model Revisited

from our normal activities and settings can open up the creative venues of the child within us, thereby making us more receptive to the things of God.

The time element of a retreat is very inviting, particularly when a congregation can spend an entire day wrestling over the direction of the Ministry of Christian education. When a night sleep-over is possible, it also enhances the experience with a powerful sense of reflection. The program format of the retreat follows much the same as the Program Planning Workshop. The only difference is more time, a more relaxed setting and a recreational atmosphere.

The Sunday Morning Introduction

Another approach for introducing the program of Christian education is during the regular Sunday morning worship. It should not disrupt our Christianity to pause for a Sunday or two and concentrate on the Ministry of Christian Education. The fruit of such an activity will be far greater than a few regular moments in worship. In fact, when are we most likely to have broad congregational representation? Yes, on a Sunday morning. The program format for this approach can remain the same as the other two. However, an inspirational message, with songs, would be a required addition.

Although many congregations initially will resist anything that departs from "regular" Sunday worship, a worshipful approach to introducing Christian education can be formulated. Such a formulation will require commitment, support, and input from the pastor and other worship-related entities. A key component to this approach is for the pastor to prepare a sermon that will address Christian education. (Some suggested sermon approaches, as well as a chapter on Preaching Christian Education, are included in Appendix H.) I believe the Sunday morning approach can be attractive.

The Contents of an Enabling Workshop

After having decided which introductory approach to pursue, the contents of the planning workshop should be considered. The contents of the workshop should include moments of retrospection and introspection. The questions for retrospection are:

* What have we been doing to fulfill the task of Christian education?
* How have we been doing it?
* What have been the strengths of our approach?
* What have been the weaknesses of our approach?
    To stimulate more of a more personal query of introspection, the questions are shaped as follows:
* What have I been doing, as a member of Christ's church, to fulfill the educational task of the church?
* Have I given myself to Christian education?
* Am I committed to Christian education?
* Could I improve on my involvement in educational concerns?

    The congregation should be led to ask these and other kinds of introspective questions.

    It has been my experience to note that there is a certain danger in prolonging the periods of retrospection

The Congregational Enablement-Model Revisited

and introspection. We have the tendency to turn fruitful dialogue into fruitless conversation. Therefore, the Director/Coordinator must be willing to listen to all, while always encouraging the progression of the workshop agenda. At some point the Director/Coordinator should focus the congregation's mind on the chief function of the Ministry of Christian Education.

At this point in the introduction, a statement of mission would be helpful. This statement should be a part of the distributed work-aids. One could possibly just state the mission of the Department in a one-liner--for example, "The Department of Christian Education will serve to embrace, direct and undergird all educational activities within the congregation, with a view toward fulfilling the church's mission, i.e., making disciples."

The organizational structure of the ministry should also be considered. (Refer to organizational chart in Appendix A.) Here lies the chief barrier in maintaining congregational interest. It is essential that no alienating personalities should occupy key roles. Christian education is about empowerment, not alienation. Although congregations have had difficulties liberating themselves from alienating personalities, there are ways of diffusing such a person's influence. One way is to use a wide variety of persons, including those already serving in educational capacities, i.e., Sunday School Superintendent(s), teachers, Associate Ministers etc. The organizational structure of the Department of Christian Education should reflect the diverse components of the congregation. The main structure should consist of a Director/Coordinator, Co-Director/Coordinator, Secretary, and Librarian. The size of the congregation and the scope of the tasks will determine whether other key persons are needed.

The Director/Coordinator, Co-Director/Coordinator, Secretary, and Librarian are essential to the work of the ministry. However, all auxiliary/ministry presidents, advisors, and other church leaders should serve within the Ministry of Christian Education. The collective leadership of the church should serve as significant shapers of the program. The welcomed input of all church leaders provides the impetus for the Congregational-Enablement Model and serves to enhance a sense of congregational empowerment. The church's leadership helps give ministry the cohesiveness and cooperative spirit so very much needed. Moreover, the input of the leaders assures the cooperative involvement of most persons within the congregation.

The specifics of committee member functions should, at least, be presented to all committee members. (See Appendix D.) Functional pragmatics need not "bog down" the workshop's agenda, for much of the technicalities involved in functions will be sharpened only through time and experience. Doing Christian education in collaboration empowers people for the work of Christian education.

A very important phase of the workshop involves sharpening the focus. To facilitate sharpening the focus, a reasonable portion of the workshop should be used in determining what kinds of Christian education activities need urgent implementation in one's particular congregation. This is usually discovered in how the congregation answers the following question: What is most needed in this particular church to better advance its goals? The purpose of sharpening the focus is to shape an educational emphasis for a stated period of time. The educational emphasis could correlate with the church's fiscal year. In fact, the emphasis ought to shape the church's activities for that fiscal year. Again, the emphasis is on sharpening the focus, having some desired objectives, or a clarified curriculum.

Clarity of curriculum does much to unify the congregation. Furthermore, no Christian education program should attempt to cover the whole of Christendom in a single undertaking. There is no rushing God's program, so we need not be in such a rush. The Ministry of Christian Education within the local church should face the task with life-long expectancy. If we are truly Christians, we will probably be so for the rest of our lives, or until Jesus comes -- whichever comes first.

I suggest that the educational focus of a congregation have no more than two major concerns, which thematically embrace the entire congregation. It would be a tremendous accomplishment to saturate a congregation with more than two major concerns. Nonetheless, a strong educational pilgrimage through one or two well-routed subjects should prove to be a weighty and worthwhile task.

The sensitive Pastor and sensitive Director should be able to discern what the congregation needs through a carefully-listened-to discussion. The planning workshop activities are certain to generate the much-needed discussion. The Director, or an appointee, should list what every workshop participant believes is most educationally urgent. The urgent concerns of each member will reflect what they believe the congregation needs most. It has been of surprising interest that the listing of participants' concerns will reveal a certain vein of commonality. In other words, certain areas of congregational interest will occur more often than others. In fact, two or three areas usually will surface more frequently. The implication is that the congregation itself is already aware of its own Christian education shortcomings. The area of concern that is stated most often should, through congregational consensus, be selected as the focus of the year for all Christian education activities. In order to be thematically consistent, every educational endeavor should reflect the congregational theme. So as to maintain a sharp focus, the Christian education emphasis must dominate the total life of the church. Whatever the church does, its members need to bump into the agreed-upon emphasis.

It cannot be stressed enough that the needs of the congregation must shape the educational emphasis. To push for ideal concerns that are unrelated to what the congregation feels will only frustrate the effort and discourage the people. When actual needs are being fulfilled, those needs have a way of generating self-sustaining energies. The congregation will live and grow through fulfilled Christian education needs. Moving from theory to practice, or from conversation to implementation, is the next major task. Setting in motion the "real" work of the Department of Christian Education is the next phase of this discussion.

QUESTIONS FOR DISCUSSION

1. What are your thoughts on the significance of planning?

2. Does your congregation follow through with plans? If not, why not?

3. Which approach to introducing Christian education works best in your church? Why?

4. Spend some time with a few members constructing a thematic thrust for Christian education.

VIII. Implementation of Christian Education Activities

Giving Power to the People Where They Are

The implementation of the tasks of Christian education generates new life within the local church. The challenge is great, but the rewards are greater. Seeing a congregation invigorated by the energy of a well-executed program of Christian education is a refreshing experience. This phase of the work should be approached with great

> "Seeing a congregation invigorated by the energy of a well-executed program of Christian education is a refreshing experience."

enthusiasm and augmented by high expectations. I hold that prayerful sincerity is difficult to smother. There are several approaches that can be used in implementing the activities of the Department of Christian Education. The approach may vary from congregation to congregation, what is critical is to meet the people where they are. Several approaches should be considered and adapted to one's particular situation. I offer a few options:

Auxiliary/Ministries Approach

Whichever approach is utilized, the assignment of Christian education activities should always find ways of involving the entire congregation. Congregational involvement can be secured through practical but creative strategies. Since most Black Baptist churches consist of a multitude of auxiliaries, or ministries, the <u>Auxiliary Approach</u>, or <u>Ministry Approach,</u> is highly practical. For the sake of grammatical flow, I will use the more contemporary term of existing ministries rather than auxiliaries.

Existing ministries should serve as the Ministry of Christian Education's primary resource for implementing the tasks of Christian education. Existing ministries provide ready-made seminar leaders, as well as other leadership personnel. Furthermore, existing ministries bring into the arena of Christian education the historical ethos of the congregation. Existing ministries are also composed of representatives from most age and social brackets of the congregation. The influence of existing ministries is a tremendous aid to the educational enterprise.

The Congregational Enablement-Model Revisited

Although some initial skepticism may occur, in terms of territorial invasion, most existing ministries will welcome the enriching change of pace that Christian education offers. Moreover, it is not only wise to utilize the existing ministries approach; it is essential for overcoming many congregational barriers.

To utilize this approach, the Director/Coordinator and Ministry of Christian Education members should divide the agreed-upon subject matter/educational emphases into manageable components. The dividing of the subject matter strengthens the congregational concept. Suppose a congregation wants to systematically examine the Old Testament writings. The Old Testament could easily be divided into manageable portions among the ministries. It would do well to allow the ministries the freedom of selecting their own topics and material only as it relates, however, to the major subject matter. Another example may be the congregation's concern for the "Church and The Family." Existing ministries could select and sponsor an area of the subject that interests them, i.e., "The Church and Single-Parent Families" or "Adoption and the Christian Community." If two or more ministries select the same subject matter, an opportunity is presented for creative collaboration. Ministries working together are always exciting experiences and do wonders for enhancing koinonia. Making optional selections may be another alternative. The Ministry of Christian Education should always exercise imaginative means of avoiding unnecessary conflict.

Give Power to the People!

Once the ministries have selected the area(s) of interest, they should begin giving attention to possible days when the material will be studied. The church's calendar should be made available to assist the ministries in thoughtful calendaring. The format on these days should be seminars or workshops. A seminar represents small groups in intensive discussion. A workshop consists of a larger group in discussion and demonstration that may or may not break into smaller groups. The difference in the two experiences is only in the size of group, not the content of the subject matter.

The selected days should be comfortably spaced. Activities too close together can give occasion for conflict with other affairs of the congregation's life. A freshly organized effort, Christian education or otherwise, will not fare well imposing itself in intrusive ways. Congregational sensitivity is a must throughout the process of organization.

A suggestion for starting the activities of Christian education is for each ministry to select at least two days when they will be responsible for sponsoring a Christian education event or activity. The events, workshops or seminars are not exclusive undertakings for specific ministries. The Christian education events are for the entire congregation and, if feasible, visiting friends. However, an auxiliary/ministry should be granted the privilege of leading devotional concerns, recreation, and refreshments. Recreation and refreshments are not always essential; they are only additional means of congregational involvement.

It should be made clear that the primary task of the ministry is to select the day and the time of the specific workshop/seminar. As stated above, the subject matter will also be of their choosing. However, it is the responsibility of the Ministry of Christian Education to secure workshop leaders, instructors, and the necessary study materials. The Ministry of Christian Education's inevitable influence on all curricula concerns assures close adherence to the church's Christian education focus for the specific year. The Ministry of Christian Education's close involvement in curricula concerns also guarantees congregational sensitivity. To secure instructors, workshop leaders, and study material too foreign, and too difficult, could injure the program with uselessness. I hold that "If we are not helping we are probably hurting."

The Ministry of Christian Education's overseeing of curricula concerns eliminates the possibility of educational distortions. The task of educating persons, while maintaining their enthusiasm, is difficult enough without adding obstructions. The American society's injury to the educational enthusiasm of common people need not be repeated and reinforced within the local church. Christ's ministry leads always to healing hurts and making whole the fragments of life. What is done to empower people must never be a tool to hurt people. Congregational sensitivity must always shape the curricula.

The Family Approach

The utilization of families offers a powerful method of implementing the program of Christian education. We might, for convenience and simplicity's sake, label this the <u>Family Approach</u>. Families are often the primary units within the congregation. Families not only make up the congregation but also build it up, keep it up--and they can tear it up. The intrinsic dynamics of family life can be fruitfully used for the implementation of a program of Christian Education.

The Family Approach follows the same procedures as the Existing Ministry Approach. The only difference would be in the locating of a family leader. Family structures don't call for the election of presidents and officers. Leaders emerge in families often by the perceived weight of individual incentive and responsibility. Also, leaders are often intergenerational, thus allowing for greater diversity in family expressions. Using the procedures of the Existing Ministry Approach, particularly in the division of subject matter, offers opportunity for lively and relevant presentations. The families within the congregation are well able to bring forth the pressing and painful needs of the local church.

A significant advantage in utilizing the Family Approach is its built-in opportunities for evangelism. The families that express concern for the vital issues of life can better attract other family members, who are not members of the Body of Christ. An excited family, particularly a Christian family, is one of the best tools for vital evangelism. Moreover, families know their family members better than most outsiders. They live with them and feel what they feel; thus, a way is prepared for the introducing of the Lord. The words of one Gospel writer powerfully suggest the use of the family approach. Jesus, walking by the Sea of Galilee, saw Simon and Andrew his <u>brother</u>. And when he had gone a little further, he saw James, the <u>son</u> of Zebedee, and John his <u>brother</u>. He healed the fever of Simon's <u>mother-in-law</u>. Another writer says, "Andrew, first found his own <u>brother</u>." Philip found Nathaniel. Another writer states, "They went from house to house." The New Testament gives credible support for the evangelistic use of the Family Approach.

The Family Approach, if not thoughtfully implemented, can also do congregational harm and injury to vital evangelism. Families live by a code that "blood is thicker than water." Such a code can shape an exclusive attitude, thereby walling out potential participants. It is here that the pastor's sensitivities are much needed. The alert pastor knows the families within the congregation. The pastor will be able to guide the Christian education efforts around the cliques and gangs of family perversions. For instance, to avoid family collusions and conflicts, arranging families in alphabetical order can be helpful. The major concern is to dilute any structures that hinder congregational inclusiveness. Alphabetizing families keep families intact, but it also gives equity to the procedures. Mixing up the alphabets is another way of ensuring congregational inclusiveness. Again, creativity must be functional. The Family Approach, however, can be utilized in very fruitful ways.

The "Uninvolved Member" Approach

Another approach to implementing the activities of

a program of Christian education is through <u>uninvolved members</u>. Every congregation has a proportionate mass of people who function in no auxiliary, ministry, staff, or committee. Here exists a harvest ripe for the nurturing adventures of Christian education. One of the primary reasons many of these persons are uninvolved is because "no one has hired them." In plainer, less Biblical terms, no one has asked them to do anything. Many of these persons are just waiting for a Jesus-person to show authentic interest in them. Some of the best lay leaders I have had the opportunity to work with were persons who, before I sought them out, were uninvolved. A genuine effort to minister to them as persons, rather than use them as instruments, could very easily initiate uninvolved members into the life-flow of the congregation. Another reason for uninvolvement is that the church has unfortunately put a high premium on some gifts, while neglecting and discounting others. Everybody cannot sing, lead public prayer, usher, or preach. Our limiting the range of appreciable gifts has done much to discourage valuable talents. Thus, within every congregation exists a mass of vital and valuable untapped human resources.

The *Uninvolved-Member Approach* depends greatly upon the congregational personality of the Director/Coordinator. The Director/Coordinator's sensitivity toward all persons goes a long way in this approach. To implement this approach, there must be an aggressive but sensitive effort toward including the uninvolved. One basically announces the need to see all persons who are presently uninvolved in any of the existing ministries or functions of

The Congregational Enablement-Model Revisited

the church. (It is interesting how many of these persons were just waiting for someone to show genuine interest.)

Setting apart a day and time for the initial meeting is the first step. The initial meeting should have moments when the uninvolved share the reasons for their lack of involvement. This segment of the meeting will prove highly fruitful for determining further the needs of the congregation. The next step should be to introduce the Ministry of Christian Education and its goals, program focus, and plans for the year. Sharing the essentials of the ministry should stimulate interest. The next step should be the expressed need for the uninvolved to share in the ministry of empowering the congregation. There is a place for everyone in the disciple-making enterprise. Utilizing the structural format of the Existing Ministries Approach, uninvolved members can develop a creative atmosphere for Christian education.

> *"In many instances urgency dictates the approach."*

The setting up of time and subject matter should follow in the order of the Ministry Approach. The only difference will be that formerly uninvolved members will be involved in giving new life to the church's ministry. Again, there are pleasant and positive fruits within the uninvolved.

What Determines A Congregation's Approach?

In many instances urgency dictates the approach. The urgent needs of the congregation may demand a more concentrated effort. For instance, old age, death, and sickness may have decimated the church's leadership. In such a situation deacons, deaconesses (in the South sometimes known as Mothers), trustees, and other leaders are painfully needed. The addressing of capable church leadership ought to be of utmost concern. The Ministry of Christian Education would do well to center its attention on this urgent need. A series of intensive workshops and seminars could bring immediate and thoughtful aid to this kind of situation.

In the absence of available personnel within the congregation, the Director/Coordinator would do well to seek outside help. The urgency of the congregation's need demands immediate action. Moreover, the congregation's awareness of the need will incite the needed enthusiasm. Bi-monthly or monthly activities should bring the desired results within one or two years. Special needs demand special actions; therefore, congregational needs will often shape the approach.

Public concerns, or social issues, can also influence the implementation of Christian education. The issues of society are forever impacting the life and direction of the church--or should I say, society inevitably impacts the life and direction of the church. Nonetheless, we live in a world that we cannot avoid. Its concerns are our concerns, although the approaches to those concerns may differ. I do not believe any issues impact the church more today than the drug issue and gun violence among African American males. Every family within our congregations has had, or is having, some experience with a drug abuser or a victim of violence. The issue of

The Congregational Enablement-Model Revisited

drug abuse and gun violence is a human concern and not just a mere public concern. Any educational ministry within the local church that fails to address these social ills fails to exist in the real world. The task of converting the public to a drug-free society is as much the church's responsibility as it is anyone else's. Jesus can still exorcise the demoniac, even the demons of drugs and gun violence. Therefore, Christian education must creatively find ways to confront public concerns.

The growing HIV/AIDS pandemic adversely challenges all of us. All of our churches have families who have had to suffer in silence and shame because of the cultural stigmas placed on HIV/AIDS. While ignorance and mis-education have fueled the crisis, the Ministry of Christian could boldly exemplify the compassion of Jesus by addressing this awful and painful pandemic.

The task of implementing the program of Christian education is a very exciting one. The approaches of implementation are influenced by many very real variables. A congregation's peculiarities and needs are ever the shapers to the approach. To be rigid in method and insensitive to needs is to set in motion failure. A few more housekeeping items are ours to consider, and then let's get involved in the discipling enterprise.

QUESTIONS FOR DISCUSSION

1. What should be considered in preparing a "conceptual thrust" statement for your church?

2. Discuss the approaches given as examples for the introduction of the Ministry of Christian education.

3. How can families assist in the implementation of the Ministry of Christian education?

4. What should be the determining factor in deciding which approach is best for your congregation?

5. What are the pressing social issues within your community?

IX. Introducing to the Congregation the Adventure of Christian Education

Giving Power to the People

The task of introducing the adventure of Christian Education requires an intentional and creative effort. The well-known saying, "The first impression is a lasting one" has resounding relevance in situations where Christian education has not heretofore flourished. Unfortunately, Baptists are smitten with the human tendency to resist the "new." There is also the concern of not wanting to take the congregation for granted. The congregation's knowledge of the activities of Christian education is not to be assumed. Moreover, the Department of Christian Education can ill afford a presumptuous posture. If the language of music could clarify our concern, we would say Christian Education demands a tone of urgency, a rhythm of consistency, and a ballad of intentionality. The congregation must be adequately introduced to the activities of Christian education, i.e., the emphases, dates, times, sponsors, (and when possible) the facilitators.

One way of introducing the activities of Christian education is to have an Introduction Day. (See Appendix D.) The Introduction Day will serve as the calendared platform to further introduce the department's decisions, projections, and activities for the year. It is a time when the specifics of the program are shared with the congregation-at-large. The Director/Coordinator would do well to encourage some thoughtful and creative activity to complement the day of introduction. Youth skits and musical presentations will offer welcome flavor to the occasion.

Introduction Day is not necessarily being proposed as an annual event, although it could be used as such. The major concern of Introduction Day is to present the specifics of the approach and educational activities and projections for the year. Introduction Day is very important because it seeks to lead the congregation-

> *"Christian Education demands a tone of urgency, a rhythm of consistency, and a ballad of intentionality."*

at-large into the educational process. Therefore, trivialities should never dominate the events of Introduction Day.

Suppose a congregation were to adopt the Ministry Approach of implementing Christian education. The task for each ministry, on Introduction Day, is to present to the congregation their Christian Education projections and responsibilities for the coming year. In between a skit or musical presentation each ministry, or a group of ministries, brings forth their respective presentations. (See Appendix E.) For example, the Church Choir chose to sponsor two workshops: one on the book of Job and the other on Christians and Divorce. The Church Choir's presentation may be as follows:

We, the Church Choir of Olivet Missionary Baptist Church, will present for our Christian Education project *two* workshops. One of our workshops will be on *the Book of Job,* the other on *Christians and Divorce*. The respective dates of our workshops will be *May 7*, and *July 7*. The time on each date will be from 1:00 p.m. to 4:30 p.m.

Another example may be a presentation from the Youth
Ministry. The Youth Ministry may want to sponsor quarterly seminars on Youth and the Gospels and on Drug Awareness. Their presentation may be as follows:

We, the Youth Ministry of the Olivet Missionary Baptist Church, will present for our Christian Education project four seminars. The concerns of our seminars will be Youth and the Gospels and another on Drug Awareness. These seminars will be presented quarterly, or every three months. The dates are February 1, May 10, July 12, and October 10. We will rotate the subject matter each quarter. The times of our seminars will be from 8:00 a.m. to 12:00 noon; lunch will be served.

In the event that a ministry is more elaborate than any of the above, simply give God praises for an enthusiastic ministry and proceed with gladness. The Director/Coordinator will probably have to give guidance in formulating some of the presentations. My advice is to be available to help but not so overbearing that you hurt.

One of the tasks after Introduction Day is to gather all the presented data and begin organizing the requested dates and subject matter within the church's calendar. Care should be taken that dates and subject matter do not conflict. The inclusion of Christian Education events within the church's calendar should reveal a significant change of events in the church's usual concerns. The lively presentations of the ministries signal the beginning of a viable program of Christian education. The ministry of Christian education has included and empowered the congregation for vital service and preparation. Whichever approach is utilized, the ministry should be owned by the people.

Another task of the Director/Coordinator is to begin securing qualified persons to lead or facilitate the various workshops and seminars. A variety of qualified persons will further enhance the educational activities. No one person should lead all the activities. The truth is, no one person can adequately treat the multitude of subjects included in Christian education. Furthermore, the most charismatic of teachers can eventually become monotonous and boring. To be bored is to give sin opportunity and frustrate the effort of Christian Education. The Director/Coordinator may also want to accent the activities of young people with recreational activities, films, or other creative and exciting enhancements. To bore the young is to lose the young; thus, creativity is essential.

To avoid a lackadaisical year in Christian education, the inclusion of a Christian Education Celebration Day can further highlight the educational program. In fact, a Christian Education Day is a welcome change from some of the tired affairs of many worn out Annual Days. The Christian Education Day could be festive as well as informing. Drawing from the approach of the congregation's implementation, the Ministry of Christian Education may want to award the auxiliary, family, or other person[s], who sponsored the most meaningful event in Christian education. Such awards/certificates may also be issued to individuals following the successful completion of a specific study or course of study. Certificates and awards can now be uniquely made to personalize both congregation and person. (See Appendix F.) The course cards given by our Leadership Training courses, the Ministry of Christian Education, and the Sunday School Publishing Board, are deeply rewarding for those seeking denominational accreditation. Using awards/certificates is a way of pointing out quality standards. Public recognition and congregational appreciation can only serve to further encourage the congregation in its educational endeavors. Recognizing and rewarding persons has an enabling effect on the congregation.

Another primary factor involved in a successful program of Christian Education is publicity. What people see is what they usually think about. Keeping the matters of Christian education before the people demands aggressive publicity. The activities of Christian education should receive widespread congregational publicity. Church bulletins, posters, announcements, etc., should all be used to communicate the "good news" of Christian education. The distractions of life are vast and many. Therefore, let not an activity transpire without adequate publicity.

Many of our congregations are not formally acquainted with Christian education. Good publicity serves to make an indelible impact. It is rather difficult to forget that which refuses to be ignored. So let not Christian education be ignored among the people, but let its light shine before the congregation, and within the congregation, so that everyone will see the good works of Christian education.

QUESTIONS FOR DISCUSSION

1. Discuss the various methods of introducing the Ministry of Christian Education.

2. How can existing auxiliaries and/or ministries assist in the Ministry of Christian Education?

3. What are the essentials of presenting a successful Christian education ministry?

Give Power to the People!

X. Expense and Evaluation

Evaluating the Power of the People

The matters of expense and evaluation are as important to Christian education as they are to any serious undertaking. To ignore the matter of expense is to cheapen that which Christ most valued, which is the making of disciples. Also, to overlook the matter of evaluation is to cheapen that which we ought to value: our time, our energy, and our intellect. Therefore, expense and evaluation should be given

> *"To overlook the matter of evaluation is to cheapen that which we ought to value: our time, our energy, and our intellect."*

Give Power to the People!

honest consideration. In fact, the matter of expense will reveal how honest and serious we are about Christian education. Likewise, the matter of evaluation will keep us honest about the objectives of Christian education.

Expenses

As it relates to expenses, we would do well to consider the words, "For where your treasure is, there will your heart be also" (Matthew 6:21, KJV). It is folly to assume that an adequate ministry of Christian education can be accomplished without monetary cost. The reality of monetary expenditures cannot be avoided when fulfilling the work of Jesus. I can think of no other staff person more vital to the local congregation, outside of the pastor, than a qualified Coordinator/Director of Christian Education. A good Director/Coordinator of Christian Education will do more for a church's ministry than the entire Music Ministry! This is not to discount the value of musicians; they are very important for the packaging of powerful worship. However, Jesus' mandate is for us to "make disciples," not choir members. A worthwhile budgetary item is the staffing and enriching of the Ministry of Christian Education.

Two considerations are prominent in the compensating of a Director/Coordinator of Christian Education. First of all, compensated personnel tend to function more responsibly than volunteers. The work of directing an adequate program of Christian education certainly requires that someone be responsible. The Director/Coordinator is the person who, in a very real sense, gives shape to the educational mentality of the congregation.

Anyone with such a weighty responsibility should be made aware of such a tremendous responsibility. A sure way of awakening a person's awareness is to compensate an individual according to the task. The Director/Coordinator's sense of responsibility is noticeably heightened when compensated for tasks performed. Also, the congregation's sense of expectation is appreciably heightened with compensated personnel. Compensation also reveals the sincerity of the congregation in assigning the task to the Director/Coordinator.

I can recall my initial compensation for serving as Director of Christian Education. My weekly, or "weakly," compensation was so nominal that it was called a stipend. I understood that the cultural resistance within the congregation did not give the pastor the support he might have needed for a more substantive compensation. Yet, in retrospect, I recall that a building project was in progress that was getting congregational priority. It's sad, but true, that many of our churches place more emphasis on buildings than building people. We want multi-million dollar buildings that people will use two hours a week, to be filled with people who are struggling to be Christians 24/7.

Second, the Ministry of Christian Education receives a much needed spark of appreciable incentive. The Director/Coordinator is encouraged through the means of compensation. An enthusiastic Director/Coordinator does much to invigorate the entire Ministry of Christian Education. Without a doubt, enthusiasm is a necessary ingredient for the task of Christian education. It is still true "that nothing great was ever accomplished without enthusiasm."

It may well be that most of our churches are not clear on an adequate pay scale for compensating the Director/Coordinator of Christian Education. Many of us are not sure because we have never tried to compensate anyone for the educational ministry of the church. In a very dated document, I ran across an interesting measure for consideration of compensation for a Minister of Christian Education. The Educational Consultation in 1960 carefully considered the salary matter and made this recommendation:

The salary of the Director or Minister of Christian Education, whose academic preparation is comparable to the pastor's and who has an acceptable background of experience, should be equivalent to at least a minimum of 65% of the pastor's salary. The beginning salary for the Director, or Minister of Christian Education just out of seminary, or who is in his first job as a director or minister of Christian Education, may be slightly less than the above recommended minimum of 65%, but by the end of the second year of service, the salary should be in an amount equivalent to at least 65% of the pastor's salary at that time. It is recommended that annual increases be considered.[20]

I clearly understand that many local churches struggle to adequately compensate the pastor. In these kinds of situations full compensation for a Director/Coordinator

---

20   0.   Marvin J. Taylor, *An Introduction to Christian Education* (Abingdon Press, Nashville, TN, 1966), p.127.

may be a challenge. However, a few suggestions may help us leap over this molehill. Compensation does not always have to come in a full salary. Since the Director/Coordinator is a part of the congregation, he or she is aware of the economic situation of the church. Remember? The Director/Coordinator is a congregational person! He or she loves the church!

Although a set salary is preferred, appreciable compensation can be made through other sincere gestures. The church can compensate the Director/Coordinator by taking care of certain expenses. Help the Director/Coordinator with gas, personal enrichment, continuing education, books, and other related expenses. (I recently completed a graduate degree by trading off annual convention expenses.) A yearly or semi-annual bonus is a noteworthy gesture. An expense-paid trip to local, state, or national congresses is another of the many ways that a congregation can compensate its Director/Coordinator. Failure to compensate the Director/Coordinator in some of way is to be negligent and ungrateful. The truth is that in the long run the congregation will be a better congregation, and thus better prepared to engage in more responsible stewardship, if it compensates the Director/Coordinator of Christian Education.

Another element of expenses is in resources, both human and material. The personnel who facilitate workshops and seminars should be worthy of remuneration. The serious and responsible church would hardly invite and utilize the services of a guest without proper remuneration. Again, where the budget is limited, creative stewardship should prevail. Workshops and seminars will require certain materials that can only be purchased. This is an expense that should not be discounted nor avoided. Resources are needed to maintain an adequate, relevant, and participatory educational program. One way of building a church library is to shelve purchased materials, in order to use them over and over again. The resources used within the activities of Christian education are fitting resources for the church library. Resources, both human and material, are necessary elements of the program of Christian education.

In essence, we are suggesting that the Ministry of Christian Education be given budgetary priority. The shaping of responsible disciples of Jesus Christ is a worthwhile investment for any congregation. God spared not his Son for our salvation; therefore, let us not spare our resources for God's glorification through our edification. We give God glory only when we faithfully do well the work of God. We do best the work of God when we know what is the best work of God. Moreover, the more doing the work, the more work can be done. Making disciples should never be cheapened, nor degraded, by low budgetary concerns and negligent stewardship.

Evaluation

The matter of evaluation keeps everyone honest about the fulfillment of desired objectives. The Ministry of Christian Education should be ever mindful about what it is, what it is not, what it is doing well, and what it is not doing

The Congregational Enablement-Model Revisited

well. Mechanisms for evaluation should be employed. Periodically, the Director/Coordinator, the Ministry of Christian Education, and the Pastor should evaluate the work of Christian education. Some of the concerns for honest evaluation should be:

* What have we done well?
* What have we not done well? Or where could we have done better?
* Have we done all we set out to do within the stated period of time?
* Did the congregation participate in the program of Christian education?
* What percentage of the congregation shared? What percentage did not? Why didn't they share? The concerns of evaluation should also include resources and subject matter:
* Did we adequately address the subject matter?
* How is such a judgment determined?
* Were the resource persons, teachers, and leaders equipped for the task?
* Was adequate time given for each presentation? Or can the time be decreased for efficient study?
* Were the materials appropriate for the congregation?
* Can better resources be obtained?

I suppose one of the most vital subjects for evaluation is the individual students themselves. The Ministry may want to allow the congregation to constructively critique the year's activities. Constructive criticisms from the congregation will only help improve the educational efforts of the coming year. The Ministry would do well to accept such criticisms as blessings. Allowing for criticism is an empowering expression of vulnerability. Too much of what we do in the name of the Lord continues without constructive criticism. Education is best improved when students and staff collaborate to improve it. The congregation should ultimately be a living testimony of the effectiveness of Christian education. The big question is always: Is there a noticeable change in the life and attitude of the congregation? Visible signs of improved discipleship are not hidden. They are outwardly manifested and celebrated. I encourage the use of mechanisms for evaluation.

In the event that "mechanisms for evaluation" are not clear, a point of clarification is offered. Mechanisms for evaluation are merely forms by which the department raises questions for self-criticism. (See Appendix F.) Such forms are simple to compose and easy to measure. The Director/Coordinator need only ask five to six questions, which pointedly address the issues of the Ministry, the staff, the resources, workshop formats, and personal/student enrichment. The measuring devices of choosing between bad, average, good, excellent, or the scale between one and ten are adequate "mechanisms for evaluation." The important thing is to secure data that leads toward self-improvement.

QUESTIONS FOR DISCUSSION

1. What are some of the important expense items that need to be considered for the Ministry of Christian education?

2. How can a church compensate a Minister/Director of Christian education?

3. Why is evaluation important?

4. What should be considered in evaluating the Ministry of Christian education?

Give Power to the People!

XI. Preaching Sermons on Christian Education

Preaching as a Means of Empowerment

One of the cultural mainstays of the African American church, particularly among Baptists, is the prominence of the preaching moment. In classic Protestant protocol, the proclamation of the Word is central to the Christian experience in most Black Baptist churches. This is not to imply that preaching is not important in other African American denominations, nor does it insinuate that all Black Baptist preachers are good preachers. It merely states a historical fact that preaching normally sets the tone in the Black Baptist church.

It has been mine to discover that preaching provides opportunity for vision to be cast and for intentional ministry to be emphasized. The wise pastor uses the preaching moment to bring to bear upon congregational consciousness those matters that are essential to healthy congregational life. Furthermore, a wise pastor should know that healthy congregational life exists where there are healthy persons, and healthy persons are normally those who strive to be more like Jesus.

When it comes to using the preaching moment as an opportunity to emphasize Christian education, some measure of skill and intentionality should shape the preaching task. Without preaching skill and intentionality, the pastor risks either bludgeoning the people with sermons of criticism and judgment or presenting sermons of irrelevance and obsolescence. I have found that in preaching I have opportunity to do my best teaching, as well as pastoral leading. Preaching provides the pastor with an invaluable opportunity to enhance Christian development and faith formation.

> *"The wise pastor uses the preaching moment to bring to bear upon congregational consciousness those matters that are essential to healthy congregational life."*

At risk of going astray of my primary task, I want to propose an approach to preaching that can be used to teach, as well as to advance the Ministry of Christian

Education. I refer to the Dialectical Model, as espoused in Hegelian thought and fruitfully borrowed in Christian didactics. The Dialectical Model of preaching that is able to use the best in biblical exposition is, ironically, a common approach among African American preachers. Many African American preachers are unconsciously dialectical in their approach, but are not always faithful to scripture. The Dialectical Model that I have found useful is not unconsciously approached, but is a very conscious and intentional effort to construct the sermon to affect congregational consciousness. It is also a model that facilitates preaching that teaches.

The central idea behind dialectical preaching is that for every obvious truth there is an obvious falsehood, or for every good there is an apparent evil, or for every claim of faith there is an idolatrous obstruction. Dialectical preaching discovers an obvious truth within scripture to probe and advance and juxtaposes it with an obvious sin reality within the human condition. My understanding of the dialectical model holds to the probing and advancement of a single idea in a sermon, rather than expounding on many diverse angles of doctrine. If people can walk away with one probing truth on which to shape faith, then I believe the preacher would have done well for that Sunday. It doesn't take long for the wise preacher to acknowledge that Sundays keep coming, and there is always another Sunday to continue the preaching assignment

As to the single idea in a sermon, the late Dr. Samuel Dewitt Proctor, an avid proponent of the Dialectical

Model, helped us when he asked, "What shall I have said when I shall have said it?" This question should be easily answered by the preacher, and if not, the preacher should not expect the congregation to know what he or she shall have said either. The stating of a single idea, or thesis, should be clarified by its antithesis. There should always be an obvious opposing reality for the proposed truth of the sermon. For example, in the sermon entitled, "The Promises of Christian Education," we can note the sermon's construction (Appendix H).

> **THESIS:** Christian education provides the Christian access to some powerful promises from God.
> **ANTITHESIS:** The lack of proper Christian education denies the Christian access to the wonderful promises of God.

The text clearly implies some obvious advantages, or promises given to those who are diligent in study. There is also the implication of an obvious opposing reality, which results in people of the promise being denied the promise.

When I preached this sermon over twenty-five years ago, I clearly was not as faithful, nor as knowledgeable to the dialectical approach to preaching. Yet, even from a twenty-five year distance I can detect dialectical tendencies. Admittedly, if I was to approach the text today, the sermon's construction would be radically different, yet the tension between the thesis and antithesis would probably be the same. Whatever we can state as

The Congregational Enablement-Model Revisited

true, we must also be able to state what is obviously false and clearly operative within the human community. One way of stating this is: whatever is obvious about God is always being deviated from in the human experience.

"Whatever is obvious about God is always being deviated from in the human experience."

The central idea must be so powerfully stated in relationship to the obvious sin-realities that a tension is created. Such tension should lead to a synthesis, or the bringing together of the thesis and antithesis. This leads to the answering of the relevant question, which logically in this sermon is:

RELEVANT QUESTION: How do we access the promises of Christian education?

A careful perusal of the sermon discovers an attempt to be faithful to the text by allowing the text to speak for itself. The text informs us that we can access the promises of Christian education if we would:

1. Be diligent, study!
2. Be a better worker for God.
3. Be unashamed of the gospel.
4. Be right in the handling of God's Word.

Throughout the sermon there is a single point being driven home, which was to challenge the congregation to consider the promises of Christian education. The obvious reality, operative within the faith community, is that too many of us have not positioned ourselves to receive the promises of God.

Another example in a more recent sermon attempt more clearly delineates the dialectical model. The sermon was titled, "The Irony of Christmas: The Needy God." The notion of God being needy was used as a rhetorical hook to draw the congregation into viewing Christmas in another light. It also challenged people to consider God beyond the normal ideas of omnipotent, omniscient, omnipresent, and omni-whatever. Using the Nativity texts, Matthew 1:25 and Luke 2:4-7, I proposed (the thesis) that God's need to reveal His love to us moved God to come to us in total vulnerability. A baby surely represents the most vulnerable creature on the planet, because of his or her overwhelming neediness.

The antithesis of the sermon holds that our greediness denies our willingness to be vulnerable, thus robbing us of the capacity to give or receive love. We would rather hold to the omni-notions of God to support a loveless image of ourselves, rather than acknowledge our vulnerability, which exposes our need to give and receive love. In outline form, the sermon looked as follows:

THESIS: The irony of Christmas reveals God's need to show His love by coming to us in complete vulnerability.
ANTIHESIS: Our reluctance to give and receive love exposes our unwillingness to be vulnerable.
RELEVANT QUESTION: How do we respond to the Christmas image of a vulnerable God? If we are to

truly be creatures in God's image and likeness, we must see where:

1. If we are to ever give or receive authentic love, we, too, have to become vulnerable.
2. Since love is often denied in the normal places of safety and security, re: no room in the inn, we are called to take the risks of love in places that are not the norm. Isn't it interesting that the church can be a great risk for many of us to really give and receive love? We have to stay vulnerable to really experience the church of Jesus Christ.
3. If we are to ever give or receive authentic love, we have to be vulnerable even to ourselves and to admit our vulnerability and forgive ourselves.
4. If we are to ever give or receive authentic love, vulnerability must characterize our worship. Note the cadence of worship in the text, "And they shall call His name Immanuel, which is translated, 'God with us.'" God with us, being in God's presence, is a cadence of worship. The wise men worshiped Him.

The sermon is used to teach an often ignored perspective on God that promotes discipleship. Jesus said, "The world will know that you are my disciples by your love for one another." A disciple is one who takes the risk of vulnerability as a means of being a witness for Christ. Most of us are familiar with the church's struggle to give witness to authentic love, primarily because of our limited understanding of God. The omni-whatever notions of

God feed our ego-driven notions about ourselves. It has been aptly noted that churches that have issues with love usually call a preacher who has issues with love.

What is clear to all serious-minded Christians is the church's need for intentional disciple making. Preaching can be an indispensable tool for making disciples for Jesus Christ; thus, it is a powerful vessel in Christian education.

> *"Some have even argued that if the preacher doesn't have anything to teach, he or she probably does not have anything to preach."*

The purpose of this book remains to advance a model of doing Christian education in the new millennium, yet no millennium of Christendom has been without preaching. A study in preaching throughout the ages reveals an incredible awareness by thoughtful preachers to use the preaching moment to teach. Some have even argued that if the preacher doesn't have anything to teach, he or she probably does not have anything to preach. It should at least be noted that a lot of Black preaching has become a tool to support the values of the dominant culture, rather than to develop disciples of Jesus Christ. Real disciples of Jesus are generally counter-cultural. They turn the world upside down. Preaching that is used to advance the values of the dominant culture ceases to be Christian, let alone prophetic. We cannot espouse the values of an oppressive culture and expect to develop people who are faithful to the gospel of Jesus Christ. In Romans 12:2 Paul said, "And do not be conformed to this world, but be transformed by the renewing of your mind, that you may prove what is that good and acceptable and perfect will of God." Preaching should always be in tension with the values of the culture, not co-opted by the dominant culture.

This brief entrance into the world of preaching was only to suggest that preaching can be a powerful tool for advancing the cause of Christian education. A well-thought-out sermon can do much to whet a congregation's appetite to learn, as well as to empower a congregation for ministry. A comprehensive treatment on the varied nuances of preaching is a discussion for another time and probably better done by another person. I am only offering what I have found useful for me as I have tried to teach as I preached.

DISCUSSION QUESTIONS

1. What are your thoughts about preaching in the Black Baptist church?

2. What do you think of the author's position on preaching being an opportunity to advance Christian education?

3. If you are not a preacher, listen to your pastor's sermon and list the Christian education emphases.

4. If you are a preacher, explore and prepare as sermon using the preaching model as presented by the author.

XII. Bible Study for Christian Education

Teaching to Give Power to the People

REALITY BIBLE STUDY:
"People of the Book"

A favorite admonition of our religious parents was to "get in the Book." They believed that careful attention to the Bible was essential to living a life of faith. They believed the contours of our life would be more in line with Jesus if we would "get in the Book." Such a faith posture operates on the belief that the God of the Bible could, in fact, be experienced in our daily lives and we could become "people of the Book."

On one level, the admonition to "get in the Book" was an appeal for consistent Bible study. It was expected that we would be better Christians if our knowledge of the Bible were ongoing. Hence the saying, "We will do better when we know better."

However, recent studies in the slave narratives revealed that our slave ancestors often spoke in coded language. Many of the terms and phrases of the slaves were filled with what linguistics calls meta-meaning. Meta-meaning messages are terms and phrases with many meanings. There is not only what is said, but also what is meant. What is meant represented the deeper meaning of the message. The deep meaning of the message was often dependent upon who was transmitting the message, as well as who was receiving the message. For instance, the story of Sojourner Truth highlights the use of religious jargon to arrange for rendezvous for emancipation. Everyone, including the oppressor, heard the message, but only those for whom it was intended understood the message. Howard Thurman's "The Negro Speaks of Life and Death" noted the deep meanings of the religious jargon employed by the oppressed as expressed in songs.

I further believe the reference to "getting in the Book" was also a codified message for our people to see themselves as "people of the Book," and not just an appeal for the gaining of biblical knowledge. In fact, access to any kind of systematized knowledge was prohibited during the slave experience. Yet, Christian instruction was believed to be essential for the

The Congregational Enablement-Model Revisited

maintenance of contented slaves. Therefore, the slaves used what was available to help them articulate the hope of freedom.

An example might well be that the lyrics in the song "Everybody talking about going to heaven, ain't going " were a way of taunting the hypocritical faith of the oppressor. The oppressor heard Negroes singing, while the slaves were giving expression to the false claims of Christianity that were being advanced by people whose lives were antithetical to the Christian faith.

> *"It is yet possible for us to see ourselves in the "Book," so that the Bible becomes a living witness to the complex issues of our day-to-day living."*

It just might be that the admonition to be "in the Book" was a residual phrase from the slave experience, which was actually a call to see "us" on the pages of the book. We were being invited to be participants within the faith drama of oppressed Israel, as God acted on their behalf. Such a witness inspired oppressed people to persevere through the harsh hell of chattel slavery, and Jim Crowism. It is yet possible for us to see ourselves in the "Book," so that the Bible becomes a living witness to the complex issues of our day-to-day living.

As I struggle with teaching the Bible in today's church, I strongly believe that the challenge of Bible study today is to overcome the deep-rooted practice of teaching the

Bible for the sake of gaining increased biblical knowledge and to get our people to see themselves in the Book. We are to do more than import oppressive interpretations of the Bible that basically seek to rationalize faith. We are to enable our people to experience the Bible and live their faith. For the Bible to become relevant to people who are living out life in a Post-modern, and some even say Post-soul era, it is important for our people to see "us" engaged in the same struggles as our biblical ancestors. Some see our age as being occupied by people with an "in-your-face" attitude. Most of the people who really need the witness of the Bible would appreciate an approach to the Bible that puts the Bible "in your face."

For one, most of our people do not have the patience or, to be honest, the capacity for disciplined study of the Bible. The complexity of studies required for approaching the study of the Bible can be overwhelming to the average church attendee. However, the average church attendee would eagerly embrace an approach to Bible study that actually touched him or her where he or she lives. If the average church attendee is engaged by the Bible in a manner in which he or she experiences the Bible living where he or she lives, then the Bible becomes more than an artifact of faith, but a relevant tool for faithful living.

I have been experimenting with an approach, which I refer to as "Reality Bible Study." Reality Bible Study approaches the study of the Bible with the intent of engaging people where they live. The recent craze of Reality Television is highly suggestive of how Reality Bible Study interacts with the average church attendee. In Reality Television average people are invited to participate in dramatic presentations without staged props, learned lines, professional expertise, or scripted outcomes.

The use of average, or common, people is attractive because it reveals that average people can fulfill the expectations of an actor. A presentation without learned lines and scripted outcomes invites the viewers to participate and in some way impact the outcome. Reality Television is a big hit because it invites ordinary people to participate in an activity that had been reserved for the trained professional.

Reality Bible Study approaches the study of the Bible by inviting the average church attendee to participate in the dramatic activities of the Bible without being a trained professional. Reality Bible Study invites the people to be in the Book, free of the baggage of learned lines and the scripted outcomes of some prescriptive Bible study model. Reality Bible Study demonstrates how an average church attendee can participate in the drama of the Bible where he or she lives. The Bible uses the historical responses of our faith ancestors to engage people in the present. Moreover, Reality Bible Study opens up the Bible in such a way that faith is developed in the day-to-day life of the average church attendee. In reality, the

Bible is not the property of trained professionals, but the book of the people, who are the "people of the Book."

Reality Bible Study begins with the assumption that whatever experience is presented in the Bible story can find contemporary expression. Although there may be cultural distinctions, the reality of culture colors the experiences within the lives of the Bible people, as well as within our lives. The Bible is brutally honest about its cultural realities; thus, we should be as forthright about ours. In the Bible there were cultural expectations for men and women, just as there are cultural expectations for men and women today.

Reality Bible Study also assumes that there are enormous similarities in the faith challenges of the Bible people and the people of our day. Israel's vacillating faith was the result of powerfully appealing alternatives to faith. Likewise, the vacillating faith of the average church attendee is the result of powerfully appealing alternatives. Reality Bible Study addresses the faith challenges of today, in light of the faith challenges of our Bible ancestors.

Reality Bible Study does not negate nor replace serious Bible study. In fact, Reality Bible Study allows us to see the fruit of serious Bible study to materialize in the lives of God's people in concrete ways.

> *"Reality Bible Study begins with the assumption that whatever experience is presented in the Bible story can find contemporary expression."*

The facilitators of Reality Bible Study are expected to be serious students of the Bible, because it takes a serious student of the Bible to help people connect the dots between the Bible world and our world.

Finally, Reality Bible Study believes that the relentless love of God is just as real now as it has ever been. The Bible's testimony of God's undying love can be experienced in the life of the average church attendee. Not even the Bible limits the love of God to the world of the Bible; it instead gives witness that God's love is "from everlasting to everlasting." The challenge is for those of us who are responsible for the faith development of God's people to make the Bible live, so that our people can become "people of the Book."

The Reality Bible Study approach can be applied to all scriptures, although some genres of scripture may be more readily applied than others. For instance, biblical narratives are probably more readily applied than Psalms, Proverbs, and the Apocryphal witnesses, such as the Revelations. Some biblical writings will require more of the facilitator in preparing a Reality Bible Study lesson. The facilitator might have to supplement some studies of the Bible with background information.

Give Power to the People!

A REALITY BIBLE STUDY LESSON

MATERIALS NEEDED: Bible, Board and Erasable markers, or Flip Chart and markers, or a Chalk Board with chalk

TEXT: 1 Kings 18:20-39

READ THE TEXT – The class participants should have read the assigned passage, or book. (I encourage reading the text at least three times, as well as writing it out.)

KEY QUESTIONS: During the asking of each question, be prepared to write each response upon the board. It is amazing what happens when people see their responses going up on a board. It gets real!

A relaxed and open atmosphere is essential for this part of the study. It is important that you, or the facilitator, allow for the responses of the individuals to shape the discussion, and not your preconceived conclusions. This is about the people "getting in the Book," and not us getting in the people.

Who are the characters in the text? Elijah, Ahab, 450 prophets of Baal, 400 prophets of Asherah, and the people of Israel.

What is the essential truth about God, or God's people, being lifted up in the text?

To get at this it would helpful to clarify the differences between the faith of Elijah, the prophets of Baal, the prophets of Asherah, and the people of Israel.

Some possible responses: Be faithful to God; worship God alone; live uncompromised faith; trust God; be willing to stand for your beliefs even if you have to stand alone.

A Summary of the essential truth: God expects total loyalty and commitment from those who claim to be in relationship with Him.

What is the tension, or conflict, within the text?
Some possible responses: Living for God is dangerous; risky; faith is confrontational to evil; government-based religion is oppressive; faith is often in conflict with the stated powers; God's people must make a decision who they will serve.

A summary of the tension: The conflict between complete loyalty to God and government-sanctioned religion can confuse God's people.

How is the specific tension or conflict within the text manifested today?
Military Industrial Complex; Multi-national corporations; economics and faith; being a Christian in a heathen world; social pressures to conform; being able to stand when no one stands with you.

A summary of the tension in our world: The conflict between what is demanded of us to sustain life and living a life of faith can be very challenging.

How do we think God wants us to respond to the tension or the conflict in the text as it is manifested in our world?

Some possible responses: Be faithful; don't run; fight not flight; organize to challenge corrupt powers; be a worshiper; believe in God's ability to respond to the faithful; trust God.

A summary of our responses: To be faithful believers, we must be prepared to confront evil, no matter how insurmountable it may seem.

Are there ways in which we "do" church that prevent us from responding to God's Word in the text?

A REALITY BIBLE STUDY LESSON
(Using a Non-Narrative Text)

TEXT: Psalm 1

READ THE TEXT: The class participants should have read the assigned passage or book. (I encourage reading the passage at least three times, plus writing it out.)

KEY QUESTIONS: There are no stated characters within this text; thus, it demands an approach that invites people to see themselves. Allow people opportunity to respond in their own way.

What is the essential truth about God, or God's people, being lifted up in the text?

Some possible responses: Blessed living is to obey God's word; we are not to follow the advice of wicked people; God will bless the lives of those who keep His Word; prosperity begins with obeying God

Summary of the essential truth: The blessings of God are assured to those who faithfully obey His Word.

What is the tension, or conflict within the text?
Some possible responses:
Disobedience, listening to wickedness instead of God's Word; listening leads to becoming; the company we keep is important; judgment will separate the righteous from the wicked.

Summary of the essential tension: The world is filled with people who will seek to lead God's people away from their blessedness.

How is the specific tension or conflict within the text manifested today?

Some possible responses: Gangs, party spirits; seeking approval of others; people more important than God; Christians making slight, but dangerous compromises; toxic relationships; living without God's Word in our lives.

A summary of the tension in our world: The challenge of ungodly relationships can lead to an unfruitful life.

How do we think God wants us to respond to the tensions or conflicts in the text, as they are manifested in our world?

Some possible responses: Study God's Word; love God's Word; avoid bad company; eliminate toxic relationships; live life for God.

A summary of our responses: In order to overcome the power of bad relationships, the blessings of God demand that our relationship to God be rooted in God's Word.

Are there ways in which we "do" church that prevent us from responding to God's Word in the text?

SUMMATION AND CONCLUSION

The above model is an effort to encourage organized and intentional Christian education. Bringing within the life of a congregation a viable ministry of Christian education is a worthwhile and exciting endeavor. I believe the Congregational- Enablement Model provides a tool for fulfilling the task of organizing a Ministry of Christian Education. A congregation empowered through this ministry will be a vibrant contagion in the area of "making disciples."

The validity of the Congregational-Enablement Approach is rooted in the New Testament understanding of witnessing, which leads to the perpetuating of disciples. Discipleship produces discipleship. Thus, the Congregational-Enablement Approach merely mirrors the dynamics of New Testament witnessing by giving power to the people.

In summary, the task of "making disciples" ultimately belongs to the entire congregation. The vehicle we use to empower the congregation toward assuming this responsibility is intentional Christian education. Christian education brings to bear upon congregational conscience the big burden of discipleship. The Congregational-Enablement Model seeks to facilitate this process.

It should be noted that the task of Christian education should never be approached expecting instant results, although some will certainly appear. It is a task that requires life-long dedication, patience, creativity, resiliency, and long-suffering. Moreover, our congregations will be the better for the faithful efforts put forth. Our challenge is to complete that which has been assigned to us. It is to this end that I share in the struggle.

Finally, I have only tried to share what I am attempting. Admittedly, my present efforts vary logistically from what I propose, but I am fundamentally faithful to the Congregational-Enablement approach. Also, I do not feel that I have overstated the possibility of this model working in most Black Baptist churches. I believe that it will work. Furthermore, I have faith in inspired ideas. I also trust the suggestions offered will further enhance existing ministries of Christian Education. Yet the major concern is for those among the multitudes who have not a viable Ministry of Christian Education. It is to this crowd that I compassionately reach out.

Let me also add that I am not seeking to impose a model upon a congregation. I am merely sharing a model with the people who have shaped considerably my life - the National Baptist Convention, U.S.A., Inc. I believe that our beloved convention exists for one reason alone: to give power to the people!

APPENDICES

APPENDIX A
A Suggested Church Flow Chart

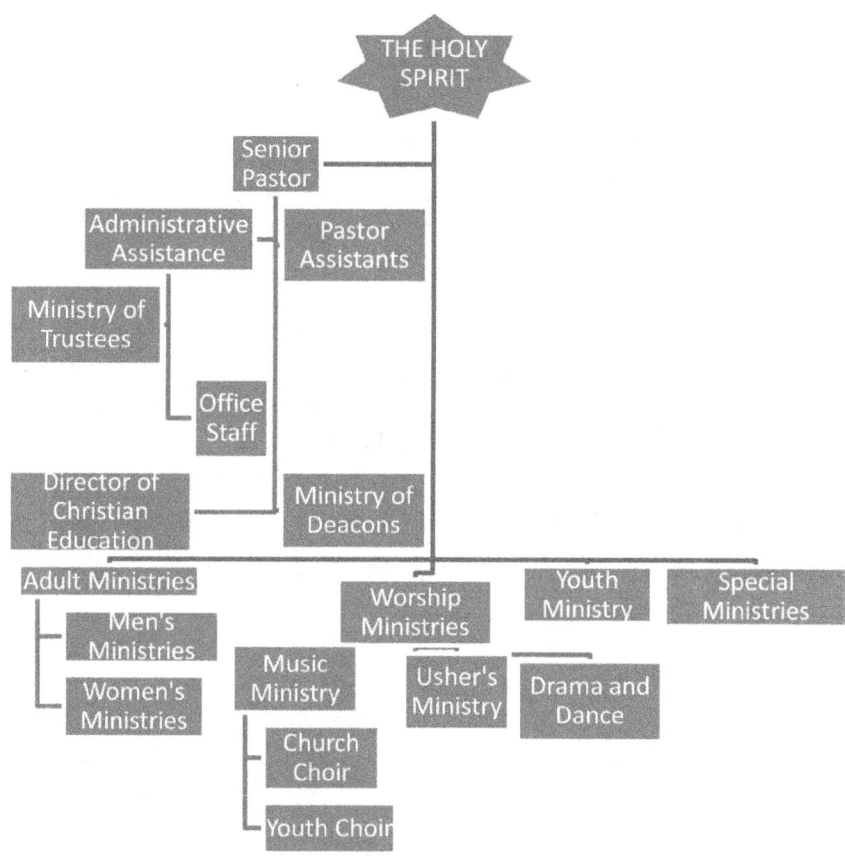

APPENDIX B
The Conceptual Thrust/Mission Statement

The need for the intentional development of Christians has led our congregation to take a specific action. The action we choose to take is the development of an ongoing ministry of Christian Education. This program will serve to facilitate our growth in the Lord. Of primary concern in the development of a ministry of Christian education, the following components are being recognized:

1. A concern for the experience of God, as told by the biblical witnesses. Such a concern is best addressed in the form of systematic Bible Study.

2. A concern for the experiences of God, as experienced within one's particular denomination, community, and congregation. Such a concern is addressed through historical reflection, doctrinal emphases, and congregational dialogue.

3. A concern for the day-to-day struggles that impact human lives. Such concerns focus upon the very real issues that currently impact our humanity, such as the family, jobs, politics, economics, sex, drugs, and secular education.

4. A concern for engaging one's Christian experiences into fulfilling the mandate of the church - "making disciples." Evangelism is always a by-product of an effective program of Christian education.

APPENDIX C

Olivet Missionary Baptist Church
Nashville, TN 37203

January 1, 20___ ....9:00 a.m.

Christian Education (CHED) Planning Workshop Agenda

I. Devotional Period Minister/Appointee

II. Purpose of Meeting Pastor
 Director/Coordinator of CHED

III. Christian Education at Olivet:
 A. Retrospection - Where have we been?
 B. Introspection - What have I done to help us get there?
 C. Christian Education in perspective - Definition

BREAK   BREAK   BREAK   BREAK   BREAK   BREAK

IV. Organizing for Christian Education:

 A. What are the needs of the Olivet Church Family? Sharpening the focus.

 B. How should we address these needs?

V. The Ministry of Christian Education

    A. In perspective (Definition)

    B. Who will serve? Selection of Ministry members and officers

BREAK   BREAK   BREAK   BREAK   BREAK   BREAK

VI. Addendum

    A.

    B.

*This same format may be used in the retreat setting, with minor modifications.

APPENDIX D

Suggested duty descriptions of the primary officers serving within the Ministry of Christian Education:

Director/Coordinator - The Director/Coordinator shall serve as that person who first leads the investigation of the concerns of Christian education. In light of such investigation, the Director/Coordinator informs, enables, and coordinates the church's educational activities. The Director/Coordinator shall be the one responsible for the educational resources, both in personnel and material. All activities of the Director/Coordinator are done in collaboration with pastoral authority.

Co-Director/Coordinator - The Co-Director/Coordinator shall serve in conjunction with the Director. This person shall assist the Director in all areas of the educational ministry.

Secretary - The Secretary shall serve as that person who records, maintains, and distributes those necessary proceedings of the Educational Department. This person is responsible for accurate and concise recordings of all the proceedings in annual, monthly, quarterly, or special meetings.

Librarian - The Librarian shall serve as that person who, upon Department approval, secures and maintains the resources of the church's Library. This person shall see that all materials are current, in decent and workable condition, and available when needed. The Librarian shall devise a system for the maintenance of a viable church library.

APPENDIX E

A Suggested format for
Christian Education Planning Form

We, the _____, will present for our

Christian Education project _____

workshops/seminars. One of our workshops/seminars

will be _____, and the

other will be _____.

The tentative dates for our projects will be _____

_____. The times will be

from _____ to _____.

_____, President/Ministry Leader

_____, Director of Christian Education

_____, Pastor

*This form is to be used as a guide on Introduction Day.

APPENDIX F
(Suggested Order of Christian Education Day)

Olivet Missionary Baptist Church
Nashville, TN 37203

January 1, 20 __ ....10:00 a.m.

Christian Education Introduction Day

Devotional Period   Minister/Appointee

Musical Presentation/Skit   Youth Ministry

Music Department

Purpose of Meeting &   Director/Coordinator
Olivet's Educational Emphases

Introduction of Olivet's Educational Ministry
Roll Call of Auxiliaries

Special Presentation (Musical or Drama)

ROLL CALL CONTINUED

DISMISSAL

Fellowship Hour (Refreshments to be served)

APPENDIX G

Olivet Missionary Baptist Church
Nashville, TN 37203

Suggested Christian Education Evaluation Form

Please be honest in your evaluations. Your evaluation helps you to help yourself and the church family.

Classes/workshops attended (state the exact classes)

_____

_____

_____

Instructors: _____

_____

How do you rate the scheduling of our workshops?
Inconvenient _____   Convenient _____

Was there adequate time for workshops?
Inadequate _____   Adequate _____

Were there enough workshops?
Not Enough _____   Enough _____

Give Power to the People!

How do you rate your instructor(s)?
Unsatisfactory _____   Good _____
Satisfactory   _____   Excellent _____

Please give any helpful suggestions that might help us improve our Department of Christian Education.

_____
_____
_____
_____
_____

APPENDIX H

SERMONS ON CHRISTIAN EDUCATION

"The Promises of Christian Education"

"Do your best to present yourself to God as one approved, a workman who has no need to be ashamed, rightly handling the word of truth." (2 Timothy 2:15 RSV)

"Study to shew thyself approved unto God, a workman that needeth not to be ashamed, rightly dividing the word of truth." (2 Timothy 2:15 KJV)

The writer of our text, a pseudonymous Paul, writes to Timothy, and to us, words of ageless importance. He writes to inform us of the need to be scholastically adept in the things heard, taught, proclaimed, and believed concerning the Christian faith. The urgent tremors by which the words flow from the writer's pen can scarcely be avoided or ignored. There seems to be a mounting crisis within the Christian community that can be corrected only through tedious teaching and laborious learning. It seems that there were then, as now, growing numbers of misinformed, misleading, misbehaving, and mischievous misfits, who would carelessly pervert and pollute the word of truth.

We cannot and must not assume that all who pervert and pollute the word of truth act out of malice. It may be that some persons' actions are due to an "absence of malice." Many times we pervert and pollute the word of truth out of blind sincerity. We just simply don't know any better. However, in the secular arena, we usually don't receive pardon if we break the law and declare, "We didn't know any better." No! The unlettered often receive harsher punishment. For there is a cruel and insensitive law which states, "Ignorance of the law is no excuse." This law has haunted all who have tried to escape punishment by way of ignorance.

I do not know all of the logic behind the formulation of this law. Maybe you of the law will find grace to share with this dull-of-mind preacher. Yet, I would venture to guess that this law was written under the risky assumption that the public availability of all law suggests that we should know better. Ignorance of the law is no excuse because no one should be totally ignorant of that which is available to him or her.

It seems out of a similar assumption that this pseudonymous Paul writes to a struggling Christian, Timothy. Maybe God assumes that Christians ought to know something about Him? Maybe God assumes that we ought to know, based upon the availability of evidence, the ways of the Lord? Maybe God assumes that the body of Christ ought to know something about the words of Christ? Maybe God assumes that we ought to know better and do better because of the many wondrous things He has done for us? I am not certain that "the Lord's thoughts are not my thoughts, his ways are not my ways," but I have sense enough to know that there is an abundance of evidence that convinces me that I have no excuse to claim total ignorance of the word of truth. You and I, like Timothy, have heard, been taught, have proclaimed, and have even believed something about Jesus! Furthermore, I don't want to risk coming before God under some cloak of ignorance, talking about, "I didn't know." God may quickly reply, "I know you not, you worker of iniquity."

Timothy had been a good student of the Word. He had received a quality religious education in his home from his mother and his grandmother. He had listened well to the lettered and learned brethren and sisters. Words of wisdom had fallen upon him from the gurus of the faith. His training helped ease the anxieties of the ever-present struggles of the church. So when he read the urgent promptings of this letter he was probably shaken, startled, and stunned.

He was startled by the urgency of the words. For the words glowed with eagerness, prompting Timothy to get in a hurry. He was probably stunned by the piercing insights of an elder traveler, informing him of things he thought he already knew. He was certainly shaken to know that right there within his congregation were persons who would pollute and pervert the word of truth.

I imagine that no word struck him more powerfully than the word "study." "Study to show thyself approved unto God, a workman that needeth not be ashamed, rightly dividing the word of truth." Careful study will reveal that the KJV has pulled out one of its poetic prizes, or surprises, by transposing the word spoudason, which means "to be eager," or "to be ready" into the word "study." I can

Give Power to the People!

appreciate this transposition because it collapses the whole of the letter's concern into one word, "study." The letter of 2 Timothy may well have been misunderstood without the inclusion of the word "study." The meaning, the intention, the urgency of the matter is glowingly expressed in the word "study."

Some of you English majors and grammatical specialists would inform us that this is an elliptical statement--an ellipsis that commands its readers, "You study." The "you" isn't stated but it is surely understood - "you study." It's like a stop sign; the "you" isn't pronounced but <u>you</u> better stop! It's like when Momma or Daddy would tell you to do something. They wouldn't even have to call out your name, but <u>you</u> had better do it! An elliptical "you" -- you study!

This is a daring command to project upon church folk. Study? Church folk don't have to study, many dangerously assume. There are a thousand and one reasons why church folk, particularly Black church folk, need to study. It is no accident that most Blacks, religious Blacks, are Baptist. History reveals that unlike Methodist, Presbyterian, Episcopalian, Anglican, and others, Baptist churches, both Black and White, did not demand a lot of study. In Black Baptist churches, a person could go a long way without ever picking up a book. Recent years have found us struggling to correct this malady. People are no longer pleased with the perpetual polluting and perverting of the word of truth. Many have recognized that we can do better when we know better.

However, many of our churches still find themselves plagued with truth perverters and truth polluters. One example is the misuse of the Word to attack preachers. It just doesn't make a bit of sense for God's Word to be used as an assault manual against preachers. It is true that there are Biblical paradigms that correct and condemn preachers who prey on the people, rather than pray for the people. But one perverts and pollutes the Word of truth if he or she uses the entire Bible for such vigilante purposes. Preacher fighters need to study so that they can become preacher supporters. You study!

We often hide behind such ill-founded assertions that the Holy Spirit will carelessly teach us. The Holy Spirit will teach only those of us who are courageous and creative enough to open ourselves up to learning and teaching. In other words, the Holy Spirit will help or teach us only if we try to help ourselves. There is a "You-study" about the Holy Spirit. Jesus taught about the Holy Spirit before the Holy Spirit became manifest in the lives of the disciples.

One of the most disturbing and unprincipled crimes of Christians has been the offense of "eisegesis." Eisegesis means to put into the word, or text, what is not there. An example could be the frequent misuse of Jesus' words to his disciples in the Gospel of John, 14:26. Jesus informs his despairing disciples that when tribulations arise, the Holy Spirit will bring his comforting words to their remembrance. We are quick to "eisegete," asserting that we don't have to study because the Holy Spirit will bring it to our remembrance. That's pure eisegesis! Furthermore, the Holy Spirit will have difficulty recalling to our remembrance something that isn't there. We must have something up there if something is to come out. You study!

The promises of Christian education seem to guarantee quality workmanship. Persons who study and learn the ways of the Lord and the ways of the church evolve into quality workers. It is rather difficult to do any job well without some working knowledge of the job. Moreover, quality work is impossible without some prior understanding of the task. Everyone ought to agree that there is a qualitative difference in having your car worked on by a shade-tree mechanic and a mechanic who is trained, bona fide, and certified. The trained mechanic has more resources at his disposal, resources of mind and material.

While in seminary I was once asked by a preacher about the virtues of going to school. I answered him using the above analogy. I told him that there is a difference between a shade tree mechanic and one trained. The greatest distinction is between the tools at his disposal. The shade tree mechanic often has only a tattered box, a few scattered wrenches, a tree in the yard, or a grassy garage. On the other hand, the trained, certified, and bona fide mechanic has an organized garage, impressive tools, jacks, hoists, gauges, and pulleys. So it is with the preacher, or any Christian, for that matter. The shallow preacher has only a few limited tools, whereas the trained preacher has almost limitless tools at his disposal. A certified and bona fide preacher usually holds a better following than one who is shallow and shady.

Christian education promises quality work from the Christian who studies. The text places "study" before the word "work." The suggestion is that work, properly done, comes after study. Study precedes work. You study; then you work!

I think of just a few who give Biblical witness of quality work after study. Abraham, father of the faithful, had to leave the narrow confines of Ur and seek a place unknown to all but God. Yet before he could get headed in the right direction, he had to learn the ways of God. Jacob had to be tutored in the judgment and mercy of God before he could become an Israel. Joseph had to take lessons in pits, Potiphar's house, and prisons before he could reach the palace. Moses had to study liberation theology from a burning bush before emancipation could take place. Joshua had to learn the right notes of faith on the horns of freedom before the walls of oppression came down. Gideon had to be schooled in military discipline before he could gain a victory. Jesus had his carpenter shop before he had a Cross. Paul had Arabia before he had Rome. Martin Luther King, Jr., had Morehouse, Colgate, and Boston University before he had a Selma or Montgomery, Alabama, or Memphis, Tennessee.

We, too, must study before we can produce quality work. Can you imagine what our church would be if all of her members would claim the promises of Christian education? If all of her members would take seriously the "you-study" attitude, our choirs would be second only to heaven's best. Our ushers would function in regimental splendor. Our training ministries would be revived. Our young people would lead their peers into the light of the Lord. The whole church would tithe and the money-raising gimmicks would be retired. The deacons would deacon and the preachers would preach. Heaven would rejoice over the workmanship of the faithful.

Christian education also promises workers who are unashamed. I sometimes sense that Christians are ashamed of being members of the church. I notice how our young ladies have young men sitting in cars, outside of the church. It just seems to me that they would be more comfortable inside a million-dollar, air-conditioned building rather than in a stuffy, wind-blown, five hundred dollar car. Folk are ashamed of church membership!

I came out of the grocery store the other day to discover a note on my car about Jesus. I was only in there a few minutes, but somebody crept up to my car and crept away, leaving a note about Jesus. Such stealthy witnessing suggests a cowardly spirit in Christians--a Christian who was ashamed of being a Christian, who was ashamed of Christ. If Jesus is to mean anything to anybody he'll be that only through <u>somebody</u>, not through any notes. The "word was made flesh," not papyrus or paper.

Christian education promises us the courage to be unashamed. When you know something you don't mind letting the world know that you know. An unashamed Christian will talk about Jesus and the church on the job, in school, in the home, and everywhere. An unashamed Christian will say like the saints of old:

You talk about a child, that sure love Jesus -
Here is one.
Talk about a child that love the Lord -

Here is one.
Talk about a child been redeemed -
Here is one.

We join with Paul and say, "I am not ashamed of the gospel, for it is the power of God unto salvation...."

Christian education promises us also the wherewithal to rightly handle the Word of truth. To rightly handle the Word of truth is a thing to which all Christians should aspire. Nothing does a despondent soul more good than to hear somebody rightly handling the Word of truth. A person whose body is feverishly wracked with pain finds comfort from the right handling of the Word of truth. A family on the brink of divisive disaster can be made whole by the right handling of the Word of truth. A prodigal son, or a wayward daughter, will find the way back home by the right handling of the Word of truth. The lonely find companionship through the right handling of the Word of truth. An evil nation can be redeemed by the right handling of the Word of truth. Our world can be saved from nuclear holocaust by the right handling of the Word of truth.

Somebody might be wondering what is the Word of truth? I speak of the Word that was before there ever was a "was." The Word which spoke and cosmic systems came into being. The Word which was made flesh somewhere in a Bethlehem stable. The Word that walked the dusty streets of Palestine. The Word that stood up in the temple of Nazareth, and said, "The spirit of the Lord is upon me, because he has anointed me to preach the good news to the poor. He has sent me to proclaim release to the captives and the recovering of sight to the blind, to set at liberty those who are oppressed, to proclaim the acceptable year of the Lord."

The Word left Nazareth and died in Jerusalem, nailed to an old rugged Cross. The Word spoke to death, and asked death, "Where is your sting?" The Word questioned the grave, "Where is your victory?" Death had no answer and the grave offered no reply. So the Word got up with all power in heaven and earth in his hand.

One day I heard a preacher rightly handling the Word of truth. As I stood sinking deep in sin, far from the peaceful shore, I heard the Word. When I heard the Word my soul caught afire. My feet got light. My hands became useful and my heart burst with joy. There is another promise received through rightly handling the Word. The text says we can be approved unto God. I don't know about anybody else, but I want to be approved unto God. I want to hear God's grace-filled approval of my faults and failures, trials and tribulations. I want to hear God say, "Brother Alvin, you didn't have good sense, but you dared to study my Word. You were not known for your intellect, but you dared to study my Word. You've fought a good fight and you finished your course. I want to approve your work. You've been faithful over little brains, small intellect, and timid training. You've been faithful rightly divining the Word of truth. You've been faithful over a few things, come on up a little higher, higher. I want to approve of your work." I want to hear God say, "Well done."

The Congregational Enablement-Model Revisited

"Giving Meaning to Life"

Text: Genesis 2:19

Life is a beautiful experience. Our vast exposures to the vicissitudes of life give opportunity for eternal gratitude. Although life gives none of us a free ride on the wheels of destiny, the cost of living is well worth the price. We have pains, troubles, heartbreaks, disappointments, setbacks, and get-backs, but through it all, life remains worth living. Oh, I know some of us have often literally adopted the posture of Job: "Man that is born of a woman is of a few days and full of trouble." Yet even Job dared to maintain his dignity, for in the midst of trials and tribulations, he says to us, "I know that my Redeemer lives, and at last he will stand upon the earth.... I'm going to wait until my change."

Life guarantees us nothing certain but death. We are guaranteed no friends and we are not exempt from enemies. We are assured of no riches and we risk a rag-tag existence. The only thing we know is that "this is life."

I suppose my concern today evolves around a series of questions. To begin, what is life? What am I to do with life? We had no say in our being born, but what can we say about our living? How may we as individuals, as a people, get the best out of life? What can I do to give life meaning?

We are all aware of the awful state of meaninglessness. The youngest child to the eldest citizen has drunk from the tasteless cup of meaninglessness. Life has a way of

Give Power to the People!

suddenly sneaking up on us, and we ask, why am I here? What am I doing? What have I done? Where am I going? And what does life mean to me? If you have not asked similar questions, you may well exist in some fantasy zone, totally out of touch with reality.

We live in an age that welcomes, seduces, compels, and attracts our lives into shapeless meaninglessness. In many respects, we are forced into a meaningless existence. Yes, we have allowed satanic influences to dictate to us what life consists of. What gives life meaning?

For some, it is the empty accumulation of material gain. We allow materialism to give meaning to our lives. In so doing we pursue, at all cost, "stuff," while our spirits are neglected. We have no few people, and I'm included, who often allow what they own to determine who they are. What a disturbing sickness! To make something and allow what you make to make you! For others, influence equals phony persuasion. For others, power equals powerless passions.

Our streets, our homes, and even our churches are plagued with widespread meaninglessness. We have folk who will openly say, "Life doesn't mean anything to me." Such a person will kill you! They will rape you! They will prostitute their bodies! They lie! They cheat! They disrespect one another! They will sell drugs and use drugs! They will sell poison and drink poison! There is an Indian reservation in the Midwest, which weekly reports teenage suicide. Young Indians, like young Blacks, have lost meaning for life and living. Therefore, they now surrender

The Congregational Enablement-Model Revisited

to a fast death. What is life? Why do some care so little about living?

The Creation narrative, as expressed in our text, offers a fascinating clue to the deep secrets of life. The celestial bodies that dignify the heavens had come to their creative conclusion. The earth revolved stark naked, with its majestic mountains, sloping hills, vacuous valleys, rumbling rivers, laughing lakes, swirling seas, and august oceans. The heavens and the earth silently serenaded the heavenly host. Trees sprang up and aimed themselves toward the sky. Shrubs and herbs meticulously decorated earth's landscape. Suddenly, with a scoop of dust and a quick gust of Divine breath, man -- humanity -- became a living being.

God gave orders in reference to the maintenance of life. God has always sent forth some "thou shalts" and some "thou shalt nots." We must never risk life by doing whatever we want to do. There are some "thou shalts" and some "thou shalt nots" inscribed on the tablets of eternity.

After God commanded us, the Lord God said, "It is not good that man should be alone; I will make a helper for him." We are quick to give this verse eternal reference to the making of woman. In fact, woman does prove to be, and yet remains, the ultimate helpmate. But other activities took place before the creation of woman.

Listen: "It is not good that the man should be alone...." So out of the ground the Lord God formed every beast of the field and every bird of the air, and brought them to the man to see what <u>he</u> would call them; and whatever the man called every <u>living</u> creature, that was its name."

Now, I'm not interested in promoting creationism over evolution. I'm comfortable with creation and evolution. Evolution doesn't shake or destroy my faith, nor does creationism question my intelligence.

I understand creationism and evolution to be answering two different questions. Creationism answers <u>why</u> it happened, whereas evolution answers <u>how</u> it happened. (I would that our young people would grasp the distinction.)

The creation story seems to suggest that life for humanity was meaningless until a helper came along. "It is not good for man to be alone." If meaningless suggests anything, it suggests being alone. If life is empty, it is because of an awesome sense of loneliness. If life seems void, vacant, and vacuous, it is saturated in deep loneliness. When life offers nothing to stimulate living, we're alone. Meaninglessness is "alone-ness." God said it is not good for us to live meaningless lives.

God did something about our meaninglessness. "So out of the ground the Lord God formed every beast of the field and every bird of the air, and brought them to the man to see what he would call them; and whatever the man called every living creature, that was its name."

Listen to the power of this text! Everything made was already made but had no names! The world was made. A fully furnished universe, but it all lacked specific names. Some of us may have missed the importance of names.

When we name something, we define its existence. Our world can only be understood by specific definitions, because when something lacks definition it simply lacks meaning. How can we understand something if we fail to give it a name?

"Whatever the man called every <u>living</u> creature that was its name." What this text says to us is that God has given us the responsibility to give meaning to our own lives. I thank God for not making me a mere puppet with no say-so about life. God says, "you name it and so it is." Whatever we name the makings of life, so it is.

I suspect that the tragedy of Blacks, Indians, and all oppressed people is that we've tried to live in a world we didn't name. The reason many of us still feel the shackling limitations of oppression is because we're living in a world not of our making. We have accepted a world that, for the most part, has been named by the Devil.

Why do you think some people succeed easily, while others die trying? Why does it seem, says the prophet, "that good people suffer and evildoers prosper?" What determines whether or not you make it in a system not designed for our well-being? Who decides whether or not you succeed? Often a people not of our own persuasion.

If we are to give life more meaning, we must name our world and live according to our names. Our theme, "Olivet Is All Right," serves notice of a people struggling to name their world. Olivet, or no other congregation, can live a meaningful life allowing negativity to shape its existence. We must name our own world, or somebody will name it for us. And whoever gives the name bears the power, for whenever you name something you also empower it.

"Every beast... and every bird brought He them to the man; and whatever he called every <u>living</u> creature, that was its name." Notice the text stresses every living creature. The concern is for the living and not for the dead. One reason so many of us have not meaningful lives is because we choose to live among the dead. We keep trying to breathe life and give life to that which is already dead.

We saw just the other day during Bible study that the reality of God's blessing Joseph was not realized until Joseph buried his hatchet against his brothers. "Joseph called the name of the first-born Manasseh, for, 'God has made me forget all my hardship and all my father's house.' We need to give our hardships the name of forgetful and give positive meaning to our lives.

All experiences, bad and good, come only to enrich our lives. God doesn't allow anything to come upon us that we cannot handle. Don't let anyone fool you into believing life is to be good all of the time. Why think we Jesus said, "In the world you shall have tribulations...?" but don't despair, says Paul, "We know that all things work together for the good, for those who love the Lord." Joseph's other son Ephraim said, "God has made me fruitful in the land of my affliction."

There will be some beasts that come in our lives, some beastly experiences. Black folk, born in the jungles of Africa, have become so spooked that we are scared of everything. White folk tame wild beasts, lions, tigers, gorillas, etc., and we're scared of garden snakes and worms. We need to accept God's challenge and name and tame the beasts of our experiences. If it is the beast of lust, name it and tame it. If it is the beast of insecurity, name it and tame it. If it is the beast of pride, name it and tame it. If it is the beast of hatred, name it and tame it. If it is the beast of selfishness, name it and tame it. If it is the beast of laziness, name it and tame it. For if we don't tame our beasts, they will eat us up and destroy us.

"It is not good that the man should be alone." Life is meaningless alone. We must not allow Satan's forces to name our relationships with one another. God has made us kindred. The problem of racism is that it is an untamed beast, which gives demonic meaninglessness to our lives. I suspect the reason for so many single parents, divorce cases, and unhappy marriages is that they have allowed Satan to define the marital relationship. We live within the foolish definition that marriage is sweet romance, instant understanding, quiet cooperation, and we'll live happily ever after. No marriage, not even that of Prince Charles and Lady Di, is free of tears, void of misunderstandings, and empty of the struggle to cooperate. Marriage is what you name it and make it, not what society assumes. Our young people need to know that a boyfriend or a girlfriend doesn't make you a somebody. In fact, you had better be somebody before the relationship or the relationship might make you a nobody.

Yes, there are some bestial people who will eat you up and destroy you. But don't turn into a beast yourself. Tame the beast with love, peace, and understanding!

We must also consider in our quest to give life meaning, we need to respect other folk's lives. Life might mean something to me and it might mean something else to you. I might name life one thing and you might name it something else. No one definition of life exhausts all of life. No one name from us is the name for everybody.

Yes, I thank God, for allowing me opportunity to give life meaning. But one thing I do know, all life comes from the Lord. Not one of us can give life, we can only <u>receive</u> life. All of life comes from the Lord. We can name it and tame it, but He gives it and He gathers it. Job said, "The Lord gives and the Lord takes away, blessed be the name of the Lord."

When I think about Jesus, he came to give meaning to life. He said, "I come that you might have life and have it more abundantly." He said, "In me is life". He said, "I am the way, the truth, and the life." He said, "When you're hungry, I am the bread of life." When you need good news, "I have words of eternal life."

Jesus gave meaningful life to a man born blind, meaningful life to the deaf. Jesus gave meaningful life to an adulteress; he gave meaningful life to Lazarus, who had been dead four long days. Jesus gave meaningful life to twelve disciples, a dying thief, and a despairing church.

He even gave His life. When Jesus died he freed us to define our lives, because on the third day morning God raised him up with all power in his hand. He says, "O death, where is thy sting? O grave where is your victory? I've got the keys to life. I've got the keys to meaning!

The Congregational Enablement-Model Revisited

I've got the keys to salvation! I've got the keys to joy, unspeakable joy. And when I'm through with naming life, there's another name, that at the name of Jesus every knee should bow... and every tongue confess that Jesus Christ is Lord...."

No wonder the songwriter said:

Amazing grace, how sweet the sound
that saved a wretch like me.
I once was lost but now I'm found;
was blind but now I see.

Through many dangers, toils and snares,
I have already come
'Tis grace that brought me safe thus far
and grace will lead me on.

"The Educated Christian"

Text: 2 Peter 3:14-18 (17-18)

The issue of education, as perceived in most churches, is full of both positive and negative aspects. Our passion for education either burns hot or is frigidly chilled. In the grassroots church, we usually discover a chilling indifference toward the mere thought of an educated Christian. We say that God, through some miraculous spiritual intervention, saturates our minds with adequate education. We don't need to do anything; God will do everything. Sunday school is out. Bible study is out. Congresses of Christian education are out. Formal education, as expressed in institutions (seminaries), can never help us. We are comfortable with a marginal knowledge of the Bible, and a so-called "good time in the Lord."

On the other hand, we have those who are overly dedicated to the educational experience. We endeavor to do everything, leaving no room for God to do anything. We impose our "smart selves" into everything, not expecting God to be there already. We are totally committed to knowing something but not trying to be somebody, let alone a child of God. We are anxiously educated, with a broad range of knowledge and the stupid belief that we know as much as God.

Both of these attitudes, or personalities, express the extremes. However, somewhere between these two extremes we find ourselves. Yes, we, particularly the Black

The Congregational Enablement-Model Revisited

Baptist Church, have ambiguous attitudes toward what it means to be an educated Christian. An educated Christian, for some, is one who is arrogantly cold and stuffy. For others, an educated Christian is feverishly on fire for the Lord, and full of some spirit. Neither of the two is practical nor worthwhile.

As we contemplate the message of Second Peter, an educated Christian takes on a more practical dimension. No form of education is worth anything if it has no practical and/or common application. No educated person is worth a hill of beans, who fails to practically apply what he or she thinks he or she knows.

The Epistle of 2 Peter is addressed to the church at large. The writer of the Epistle is peculiarly interested in the behavior of Christians. It appears that folks in the church, Christians, were misbehaving. A widespread lawlessness was wreaking havoc in the church. We might say that the Christian congregation was disrespecting and disregarding what all that they <u>knew</u> to be Christian.

I suppose the greatest tragedy was the use of Scripture by licentious folk to misguide good-intentioned folk. The great tragedy of Christianity is the misunderstood freedom of the Spirit. We are strangely members of a church that encourages lawlessness. Sadder yet, we support and follow leaders who are as immoral as Satan himself. Have we not learned that there are such beasts as false prophets and phony preachers? With God as my witness, I must tell you that every preacher preaching is not of God! The easiest con in the world is to put on clerical garb, put a Bible under one's arm, and say God has called me to preach. Folk are dangerously gullible to religious con. As the writer of 2 Peter warns the Christians of his day, let me warn you that anybody can fake preaching and not all preachers preaching have been called to preach.

The concern, however, is to understand what it means to be an educated Christian. If our faith addresses that which is of eternal significance, we must never take it lightly. The Christian faith deserves whatever learning is available, if it increases our witness. In fact, any faith that is wholesomely religious deserves soundness of mind. Our faith not only deserves a measure of mind muscle, it requires such. How can we witness for the Lord if we know not the story? How can we behave in the church if we have no knowledge of Christian behavior? An educated Christian is one who respects and regards lawfulness. An educated Christian gives stability to the Christian witness.

Our world is fickle enough, without adding to its instability a fickle church. The reason young people exodus from the church, upon reaching the age of accountability, is because of the fickle nature of most churches. The continuous inconsistencies within the local church are a big turn-off to the young. Personally, there's not much church folk can/cannot/will/will not do that will rattle my faith. You might surprise me, but you won't shake my faith in God. Like the songwriter, "I've come too far from where I started from to turn back now." But it hurts me to the very depths of my soul to witness grown folk foolishly destroy young people.

How do we destroy them? Well, when we disrespect what we believe to be essential to the Christian Faith --

love for one another. When we disregard a high standard of decency and morality. When we ignore stated rules and regulations. The church has some implied rules and regulations. No, the rules are not necessarily printed on paper. (Even that wouldn't make much difference to some of us, if our blatant disregard for no smoking signs in Olivet is a sign.) But there must be some measure of consistency, if leadership is to be respected.

When our young people can witness us doing what we know is right to do, then better persons they become. Some of us are so into doing whatever we want to do that we make the church a big "trip." It is sickening the way some of us carry on in the church. We have some who are so licentious that the church is used as the arena for adulterous affairs. Yes, folk, men and women are using the church to cheat on their wife or husband. Young people, the church is not a religious dating game. The foolishness of grown-ups is wrong and we must pay for it.

The church is in need of stability, the kind that only the educated Christian brings. We can no longer risk heaven raising hell on earth. The church must turn the corner of blatant lawlessness. We must, for our sakes, put restraints on just doing what we want to do.

What, then, is an educated Christian? How might we gather in responsible mass? What is necessary for the continuation of our educational process? To whom should we look for such needed instruction?

The writer of our text gives us all we need to be educated Christians. A warning is first sounded: "You therefore, beloved, knowing this beforehand, beware lest

Give Power to the People!

you be carried away with the error of lawless men and lose your own stability" (2 Peter 3:17-18, RSV). A warning is given that faces head-on the reality and the results of lawlessness. As I have already suggested, lawlessness is a reality in the life of the church. Also, lawlessness has the damnable ability to destroy stability. Olivet Church! Instability is an issue we need to avoid.

Listen further: "But grow in grace and knowledge of our Lord and Savior Jesus Christ." We are encouraged to grow. I've been led by God to speak these past weeks on growth, Christian growth. The tragedy of a lack of growth is immaturity and infantility. Where there is no growth, immaturity and infantility are guaranteed. The lack of growth insures inept childishness. A stable church is a growing church. A stable Christian is a growing Christian. A growing Christian is an educated Christian.

There's no such thing as a full-grown, already arrived, fully bloomed Christian. Christians grow! We are eternally in the growth process. Education, or being educated, is grasping the continuous need for growth.

The writer leaves us not in the dark. There is substance to our growth. He says, "Grow in the grace and knowledge of our Lord and Savior Jesus Christ." Growth for the Christian takes place in a universe fertilized by grace. Grace, the unmerited, undeserved, "Big Favor" of God, gives us room in which to grow. We need room to grow, and grace guarantees us room. Not just any kind of room is given us, but the grace of God, as expressed and embodied in Jesus Christ.

The church, for all practical purposes, is a community of grace. We are people of grace. We are here because of the grace of God. No one of us is so important that we just have to be here. The church, Olivet, can get along well (maybe better) without me and without you. But we are here because of the grace of God. God's grace guarantees the church a continuation of existence. We come and we go, but God's truth keeps marching on. An educated Christian realizes the facts of grace. The educated Christian has accepted the truth that salvation comes only by the grace of God. The foolish, immature, childish Christian believes he or she is good for God and the church. But the educated Christian internalizes God's grace.

Grace is not left for us to loosely ponder. The writer suggests that the grace of God is best understood in the knowledge of our Lord and Savior Jesus Christ. We understand the grace of God by growing in the knowledge of our Lord and Savior Jesus Christ. In other words, grow in grace and in knowledge. If grace is to be appreciated, knowledge of Jesus must be articulated. I suspect that some of us have what Dietrich Bonhoeffer calls "cheap grace." Cheap grace comes from not knowing the facts of our Lord and Savior. Cheap grace permeates our congregations! Folk are just cheap! I speak not of monetary cheapness (although that's a spiritual reality, too). I speak of spiritual cheapness, church cheapness. Cheap grace!

However, cheap grace is avoided when we know and grow in the knowledge of our Lord and Savior. The knowledge of Jesus is not mere book knowledge. The knowledge of Jesus being suggested is a personal communion with Jesus. "Know the Lord for yourself." Such a personal communion must necessarily involve a personal commitment to live with Jesus, suffer with Jesus, die with Jesus, and rise with Jesus. Such a communion, a personal communion, means to stand for what Jesus stood for. Harry Emerson Fosdick once said, "The reason we don't stand for something is because we fall for everything." Jesus stood for what we often love to avoid -- the brotherhood and sisterhood of humanity and the fatherhood of God.

An educated Christian grows in the knowledge of Jesus Christ.

Notice what Jesus meant to the writer. Jesus was and is no mere object of adoration. Jesus is viewed as someone extremely more powerful than a good reason for a religious love song. Jesus' person and purpose are not cheapened with weak titles. Jesus is identified for what and who he is. Listen again: "Grow in the grace and knowledge of our Lord and Savior Jesus Christ." Jesus is called both Lord and Savior.

A Lord is one who exercises authority over one's subjects. The title Lord denotes the authority of Jesus. An educated Christian understands the authority of Jesus Christ. When Zacchaeus, the little man, met Jesus, he surrendered to the authority of his Lordship. He said, "Lord, the half of my goods I give to the poor." In other words, Jesus has authority over earthly possessions, so says the educated Christian. When the thief was dying on the cross, he cried out, "Lord, remember me when thou comest into thy kingdom." Jesus has authority to give salvation. On the third day morning, I hear the women testifying. "The Lord has risen..." Jesus has authority even over death.

The educated Christian surrenders to the Lordship of Jesus Christ. The second title gives the reason for such humble surrendering. Because of the second title, we can live under the first title. Not only is Jesus Lord, but Jesus is our Savior. Because Jesus saves us, He is able to lead us. Because Jesus frees us, He is able to own us. Because Jesus rescues us, He is authorized to reclaim us. Because Jesus delivers us, He is obligated to direct us. Because Jesus heals us, He is responsible to help us. Because Jesus picks us up, He is duty-bound to keep us up.

The educated Christian understands Jesus as Lord and Savior. The educated Christian church says, like the songwriter, "Growing together, loving one another, Growing together in the Lord."

The educated Christian says indeed:

All to Jesus I surrender,
I will ever love and trust him,
In His presence daily live,

I surrender, I surrender all.
All to thee, my blessed savior,
I surrender all.

THE AMAZING TEACHINGS OF GOD

"Then the proconsul believed, when he saw what had occurred, for he was astonished at the teaching of the Lord." (Acts 13:12 R.S.V.)

In an age of high technology and soaring intellectualism, the amazing teachings of God have, for the most part, received little attention. Our society with its computerized culture and "sci-fi" mentality has overlooked the vast treasures only discovered in the teachings of God. In fact, many of our colleges and universities are staffed by atheistic professors and agnostic administrators. We have people teaching our young who neither know nor serve God. Many of our professors, Black professors, who were sent to college on the crumbs and change sacrificed by some Bible-toting, God-fearing, church-going parent and/or grandparent have relegated the amazing teachings of God to the dusty shelf of insignificance. We've become so smart that the Bible is often experienced only in games and game shows called Biblical trivia.

Oh, I'm aware of the recent surge of home and church Bible study groups. I know that the American nation recently has become interested in Bible study. However, much of our newfound interest is the result of the craze of right-wing Christian conservatism. The wicked, White hate-lash of conservative Christians has fueled many, Whites and Blacks, to try and read themselves upon religion. America somehow believes it possible to read themselves upon and into the pages of sacred history, hence guaranteeing America a favored seat in God's kingdom.

But I must warn America and you, the Olivet Missionary Baptist Church, we can't read ourselves into sacred history. We will never be, nor should we desire to be, some pseudo-Israel. We are who we are, and God is who God is, and we must free ourselves from trying to mass produce "book religion." We, as a people, must come into existential contact with the amazing teachings of God. God must become real for us.

Let no one believe that I'm against Bible study. Oh yes, we must study the Bible because it contains a great library on the teachings of God. We must continue to study the Bible and we should increase our study of the Bible. But I am against the phony notion of people surface reading a few lines and becoming self-taught experts in the teachings of God. Many of us read two or three chapters and get religion. I'm against such surface study and pseudo/phony religion, which has its strength and being in spitting out a few well-memorized verses at convenient moments.

Maybe I should applaud the effort of people becoming exposed to the Bible, however slight and superficial such exposure appears. Maybe I should shout for joy at any feeble effort to learn God's words. But I can't applaud, and my heart finds no joy because my people, Black people, are being slain because of a lack of knowledge.

In our early days, the Black church used wisely the fragmented morsels of Biblical knowledge it possessed. However, the times have become too complex and too sophisticated for such fragments to sustain us. Biblical illiteracy is at an all-time high in most of our Black churches,

Give Power to the People!

Olivet included. Very few children know the books of the Bible, or any of its major characters. Our children wouldn't know a psalm from a proverb, a parable from a pun, joke from Job, riddle verses from Revelation. The reason they don't know is because we don't know; therefore, they can't know.

If the church is to regain any relevancy in the lives of our people, we must reacquaint ourselves with the amazing teachings of God. After much prayer, serious meditation, and deep reflection, the Lord has shown me His will and way for the Olivet Missionary Baptist Church. The Lord wants us to rediscover our mission in evangelism and Christian education. We must become an evangelistic church that reaches out and teaches in, so that we might maintain those who are evangelized. The time is out for people joining one Sunday and leaving the next Sunday. The time is out for people coming into the church and assuming a comfortable seat on the pew of non-involvement. The time is out for a few aggressive folk leading the church, unguided and untaught by the Holy Spirit. The time is out for investing in associations and conventions, without receiving the slightest return from one's investment. We must receive associational and conventional dividends or we must stop such careless, unprofitable investment and involvement. The time is out for high-shouting and low-living, floor-rolling and no-knowing. We must become an evangelistic and Christian educational missionary Baptist Church.

We can find in the story of our text stimulating suggestions for the mission of the church. But what I find most intriguing and interesting is the proconsul's amazement at the teachings of God. The story begins by picturing Barnabas leading Paul, guided by the Holy Spirit, in evangelism. Notice, Barnabas is leading Paul. We all know Paul to be one of the foremost leaders in the Early Church (or, we should know). But before Paul could lead, he had to be led. We find the old saying true in Paul's day, as it is true in ours: "You can't teach what you don't know and you can't lead where you don't go." The tragedy of many of our churches centers on leadership that failed in followship. From the pulpit to the pew, from the pastor to the usher, folk are running our churches without ever learning the first thing about following. People are teaching others who haven't learned anything themselves. Paul followed Barnabas before he led anybody. And the Holy Spirit led both of them.

We have accused the Holy Spirit of guiding us into some of the most ill-advised and thoughtless activities. We have blamed the Holy Ghost for our own inadequacies and insufficiencies. We'll do anything, sometimes with good intentions, and say, "We were led by the Spirit." You know, sometimes, we are victims of the devil. "The Devil makes us do some things."

However, there are within the activities of the Holy Spirit amazing teachings. There is an instructional dimension of the Holy Spirit. The Holy Spirit gives us not only soul but sense! The Holy Spirit not only touches us but teaches us! The Holy Spirit gives us not only burning, but learning, soul and sense! We are touched and taught! We receive burning and learning!

Give Power to the People!

I had many people question my sanity in pursuing ministerial studies. Some folk thought, and probably still do think, I was crazy because I spent many years in Bible and theological training. "What are you going to do with such training?" I was asked. I truthfully answered, "I don't know." And I don't know what I'm going to do with much that I've learned. But I'd rather have it and not need it than need it and not have it. I early discovered an amazement about the teachings of God.

As Paul followed Barnabas on their missionary journey, they were met by a man named Bar-Jesus, whose real name was Elymas, the magic man. Isn't it strange that Elymas, the magic man, disguised himself with the name Bar-Jesus, which means "Son of Salvation?" He was a man of tricks and traps, deceit and disguise, evil and unrighteousness. He was a perverter of the Word of God. Elymas, the magic man, had established himself in the governor's house. He was clothed and fed through government subsidies. He probably received tax exemption through fake and fraud, ministry with non-profit status.

Isn't it strange that Elymas disguised himself with the name Bar-Jesus? But if we were to engage in mission like Barnabas and Paul, we would discover in our world a lot of Elymases. Oh, I'm certain that if we would step out on the amazing teachings of God, some Elymas would attempt to obstruct our path. We have a lot of people in our communities, even our churches, with sainted names, who trick and trap, deceive and disguise, who are evil and unrighteous, and who make crooked the straight paths of the Lord.

The Congregational Enablement-Model Revisited

Black people have always been good game for tricksters and trappers. In my home community, among sister churches in California, Elymas, with the sainted name of Rev. Jim Jones, tricked and trapped Black families and friends. But not only have white Elymases, such as Jim Jones, deceived and misled our folk; we've had Black Elymases, like Prophet Jones, Daddy Grace, and Father Divine. Black men, with sainted names, tricked and trapped members of the Black community into destruction. The greater tragedy revolves around the fact that most of the tricked and trapped people come out of the Black Baptist Church.

Although Elymas does exist, we must train our folk to go into the world and un-trick the trickster and un-trap the trapsters with the amazing teachings of God -- "To be wise as a serpent but gentle as a lamb."

The Bible says Paul, who had soul and sense, who had been touched and taught, who had learning with his burning, filled with the Holy Spirit, looked on Elymas and called him by his name. Before Jesus exorcised Legion from the Gadarene man, he had to find out his name. When he identified the devil, he said, "Legion, come out of the man." Paul called Elymas, "You son of the devil, you enemy of unrighteousness, full of all deceit and villainy, will you not stop making crooked the straight paths of the Lord?"

When we've been educated in the amazing teachings of God, we are able to correctly identify the devil. If we are able to correctly identify the devil, we might begin fighting the devil and quit fighting ourselves. Church folk waste too much time fighting one another while the devil runs loose and wild.

Paul put his eyes on the devil and put a hurt on Elymas. The Bible says, "Elymas was struck [as] blind" as the darkness he taught. And the same people he led in darkness would now lead him into light.

Again, the part that intrigues and interests me is that the proconsul believed not because the choir sang, the preacher preached, the deacon prayed, or the usher reached; he believed because he was amazed at the teachings of the Lord. The proconsul was a learned man. He had been taught and tutored by the sages. He had sat at the feet of the learned and trained, but he had been tricked and trapped by Elymas. He had been deceived and disguised. He had never been a witness to the amazing teachings of God.

I wonder this morning how many here have ever been amazed by the teachings of God? I wonder this morning how many know about the amazing teachings of the Lord? At the risk of oversimplification, I want to tell you this morning about the amazing teachings of the Lord. I know some of you have heard it before, but just maybe you didn't pay close attention. So I want to put in a nutshell the essence of the amazing teachings of God.

The teachings begin with <u>God</u>. "In the beginning God...." Before there was a where and a when. Before there was what, a why, an if and a but, then or there, a now or a then. "In the beginning <u>God</u> created the heavens and the earth. The earth was without form and shape, it was void and vague. Darkness was upon the face of the deep; and the Spirit of God was moving over the face of the waters."

God spoke, light shone bright. Light became day and dark became night. God set the sun a-blazing in the sky, as the governor of the day; the moon would serve as the potentate of the night. The stars would navigate the heavens. Universes and constellations would orbit the heavens.

God spoke and the mountains bulged; valleys sank. The trees began reaching for the sky. The ocean and river beds were no longer dry. Animals took residence on the land. The fish developed gills and began to swim. The birds made highways on the airwaves. But then God made man, male and female.

God breathed life into man's soul, life to build and life to destroy. Man could soar the heights of technology, male and female. Humanity could build bridges to span the tides. Humanity would create planes to travel the skies. Humanity could make music that rivaled the melodies of the lark. We have the capacity to have a walking library in our heads, a noble republic in our hearts, and a sanctuary in our souls.

God created us in His own image, but we failed, failed, and failed. Law couldn't save us, prophets couldn't save us, synagogues couldn't save us, churches couldn't save us, and holy books couldn't save us. We tried to make ourselves greater than God. We failed, failed, and failed.

Yes, we sank deep,
>deep in sin,
>far from the peaceful shores;
>very deeply stained within,
>sinking to rise no more.

But God did not leave us there. Isn't it amazing how the Lord provides? God sent His only begotten Son. Jesus was born in a lowly manager. Jesus was raised in the ghetto of Nazareth. Jesus walked the dusty streets of Palestine, giving sight to the blind, speech to the dumb, hearing to the deaf, life to the dead, peace to the poor, hope to the oppressed, dignity to the downtrodden, and comfort to the upset.

He was misused by His friends, forsaken by His family, betrayed by the disciples, beaten by a mob, slapped by soldiers, tried by Pilate, and crucified on a Cross. But He didn't lose a thing. He kept right on giving. He gave forgiveness to His enemies, paradise to a thief, confession to a centurion, His mother to John, and He died in agony.

God raised Him up. He gave light to the world and joy to the church, for He has all power in His hand. I'm amazed by the teachings of the Lord.

You might not find it amazing, but I must say the story becomes my story --

>When   Adam's fall became my fall;
>When   Noah's ark became my ark;
>When   Abel's death became my death;
>When   Abraham's call became my call;

When	Isaac's sacrifice became my sacrifice;
When	Jacob's struggle became my struggle;
When	Joseph's dream became my dream;
When	Moses' wilderness became my wilderness;
When	Joshua's Jericho became my Jericho;
When	Samuel's Ebenezer became my Ebenezer;
When	David's music became my music;
When	Solomon's wisdom became my wisdom;
When	Jeremiah's fire became my fire; when His Balm became my Balm;
When	Isaiah's Prince of Peace became my Prince of Peace;
When	Micah's mercy became my mercy;
When	Hosea's love became my love; and when Jesus' Cross became my Cross and his resurrection my resurrection; now I can say: Blessed assurance Jesus is mine! O What a foretaste of glory divine! Heir of salvation, purchase of God, Born of His Spirit, washed in His blood. This is my story, this is my song, Praising my Savior all the day long.

Give Power to the People!

www.ingramcontent.com/pod-product-compliance
Lightning Source LLC
Chambersburg PA
CBHW072000290426
44109CB00018B/2079